WATERSI

In Worc

WATERSIDE WALKS

In Worcestershire

Richard Shurey

COUNTRYSIDE BOOKS
NEWBURY, BERKSHIRE

First published 2000

COUNTRYSIDE BOOKS
3 Catherine Road
Newbury, Berkshire

ISBN 1 85306 612 5

To view our complete range of books,
please visit us at
www.countrysidebooks.co.uk

Designed by Graham Whiteman
Photographs and maps by the author

Produced through MRM Associates Ltd., Reading
Printed by J. W. Arrowsmith Ltd., Bristol

Contents

Area Map Showing Location of the Walks

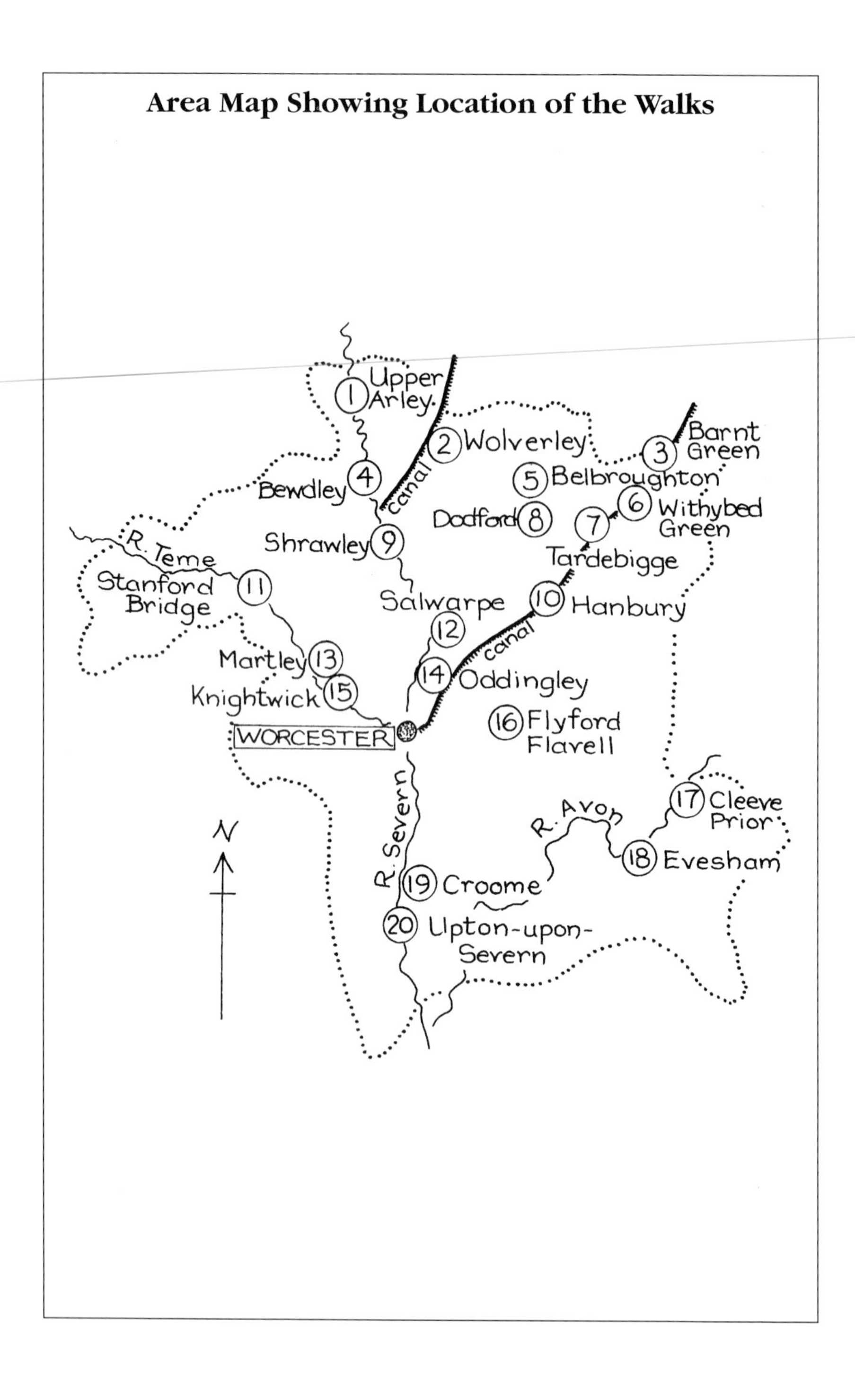

Walk

Publisher's Note

We hope that you obtain considerable enjoyment from this book; great care has been taken in its preparation. Although at the time of publication all routes followed public rights of way or permitted paths, diversion orders can be made and permissions withdrawn.

We cannot, of course, be held responsible for such diversion orders and any inaccuracies in the text which result from these or any other changes to the routes nor any damage which might result from walkers trespassing on private property. We are anxious though that all details covering the walks are kept up to date and would therefore welcome information from readers which would be relevant to future editions.

INTRODUCTION

Worcestershire is one of Britain's landlocked counties so these walks cannot take us along spectacular coastal paths. However, there is a great variety of water in this very scenic county and several of the kingdom's mightiest and loveliest rivers (the Avon, the Teme and the Severn) meander unhurriedly.

Many ancient settlements were sited along these rivers and they were both highways and barriers from early Roman days. They provided a strategic link with the outside world and a defence against attack. Worcestershire towns such as Upton-upon-Severn and Bewdley were great inland ports with all the infrastructure that entailed. The Severn became a busy trade route and many fortunes were made by plying with specially built craft which could navigate the shallow waters.

It was the Roman invaders who created the very first canal in Britain – the Fossdyke. The first modern canal in England was the St Helens Canal in Lancashire which received its Parliamentary approval in 1755 and was primarily to carry coal. The Canal Age lasted about a hundred years and at its heyday there were about 4,000 miles of navigation. Worcestershire has many uplands and high plateaus so there were great engineering feats to establish suitable routes for the county's canals. Long tunnels were sometimes the answer – one on the Worcester and Birmingham Canal had to be almost a mile and a half long to take craft through the Wast Hills.

Then there are long flights of locks (58 in only 15 miles on the Worcester to Birmingham). The Tardebigge lock is one of the deepest in the land.

These waterways, long ago abandoned by commercial traffic, are now wonderful escape routes to speedily get deep into the heart of the country. They are great worlds of nature and the towpaths are waiting to be explored by ramblers.

Sadly, some waterway routes have completely reverted to nature and been lost. However, in Worcestershire the Staffordshire and Worcester (engineered by the great James Brindley) and the Worcester and Birmingham are in good condition. The Salwarpe Canal near Droitwich which was built to convey the important commodity of salt in 1767 is being restored by enthusiasts.

Canals need a great amount of water and vast reservoirs were constructed; the Bittell Reservoirs in the north of Worcestershire were necessary to lift craft over 400 feet to the Midlands plateau. Besides pleasing the walker around their shores these waters provide sport for the sailor and angler.

Finally in our search for waterway routes there are other pools created by man; these were unashamedly to provide attractive vistas in the grounds of great country estates, as in the splendid Croome Park in the south of the county.

The 20 walks in this book are all circular, giving an opportunity to explore the surrounding area when they leave the waterside. They are between 2½ and 5½ miles in length and are all well within the capacity of the average person, including those of mature years and families with young children.

Sketch maps are provided to guide you to the starting point and give a general idea of the route to be taken. It is always a good idea to have an Ordnance Survey map with you as well – these are particularly useful for identifying the main features of views – and I have given the number of the relevant Landranger (1:50 000) sheet for each walk.

For refreshment purposes, I have suggested a pub either on the route or close by – although in some places, for example Bewdley and Evesham, you are spoilt for choice! Telephone numbers are provided so that you can check opening times and menus in advance if you wish. I have also given details of where you can park your car while you walk; if you choose a roadside option please consider local people and be careful not to obstruct any entrances or exits.

In addition to what you may see en route, I have mentioned places of interest that are within an easy drive of the walk route in case you want to plan a longer outing.

I hope that the walks will give a good contrast and great pleasure. Happy Worcestershire waterside walking!

Richard Shurey

WALK 1

UPPER ARLEY: RIVERSIDE WALKING FROM AN OUTPOST VILLAGE

Upper Arley has been called 'the extreme outpost of the county' and on this walk we sneak a few steps out of Worcestershire and into Shropshire. The peace of the Severnside is delightfully disturbed every so often by the steam trains of the Severn Valley Railway.

The River Severn near Upper Arley

Travellers once came to Upper Arley for the river crossing. The village (many said) would be spoilt by the replacement of the 'large and commodious ferry boat (complete with cabin, fireplace and chimney stack)' by a bridge.

The bridge has now arrived and Upper Arley remains a delight with the cottages and gardens below steep banks looking across to the hills on the other side of the river. The trim church has much from centuries going back to 1400; the sturdy tower is from the 16th century. Inside is a figure of a cross-legged knight. Poor Sir Walter de Bohun was celebrating his marriage at Southampton (whilst awaiting embarkation to the Holy Land) by taking part in a tournament. Perhaps trying too hard to impress his bride, Sir Walter was killed; he was brought home to Upper Arley to be buried.

Not far away was the manor which was taken down in the middle of the 19th century and replaced by a castellated mansion. This in turn was demolished in 1962.

There is still a little shop in the village which can supply goodies for a riverside picnic. The village once had two inns – one each side of the river. The Valentia Arms inn (the Earls Valentia were a local family with memorials in the church) was described in a guidebook as being 'snug and pitch piney and like a Scottish shooting lodge'. Sadly, this welcoming hostelry has now closed but the Harbour Inn on the west bank of the Severn continues to quench thirsts.

The name may seem strange for a pub so far from the coast but one remembers that the Severn was once a great commercial waterway and Upper Arley was the place where cargoes were unloaded to avoid paying taxes at Bewdley a mile or so downstream.

The Harbour Inn dates from 1512; it is a freehouse and serves a good array of beers including M & B and Bass. There is an attractive garden and plenty of space for youngsters to play. Nearby is a station of the Severn Valley Railway where magnificent steam trains operate. Meals at the Harbour Inn are the ones that walkers with a good appetite appreciate and I can recommend their steaks – with those naughty chips of course! The pub is open from 11am to 3pm and 6pm to 11pm Monday to Saturday and from 12 noon to 10.30pm on Sunday. Telephone: 01299 401204.

- **HOW TO GET THERE:** Take the B4194 from Bewdley. Within 3 miles take a lane on the right to the river.
- **PARKING:** There is a car park (fee paying) just past the Harbour Inn.
- **LENGTH OF THE WALK:** 5½ miles. Map: OS Landranger 138 Kidderminster and Wyre Forest area (GR 765800).

THE WALK

1. From the car park turn right to cross the footbridge over the River Severn. Turn left to pass the shop and post office. Go by the ramp of the old ferry terminal. Within a few steps bear left (signed to a car park). On the right was the old Valentia Arms Inn.

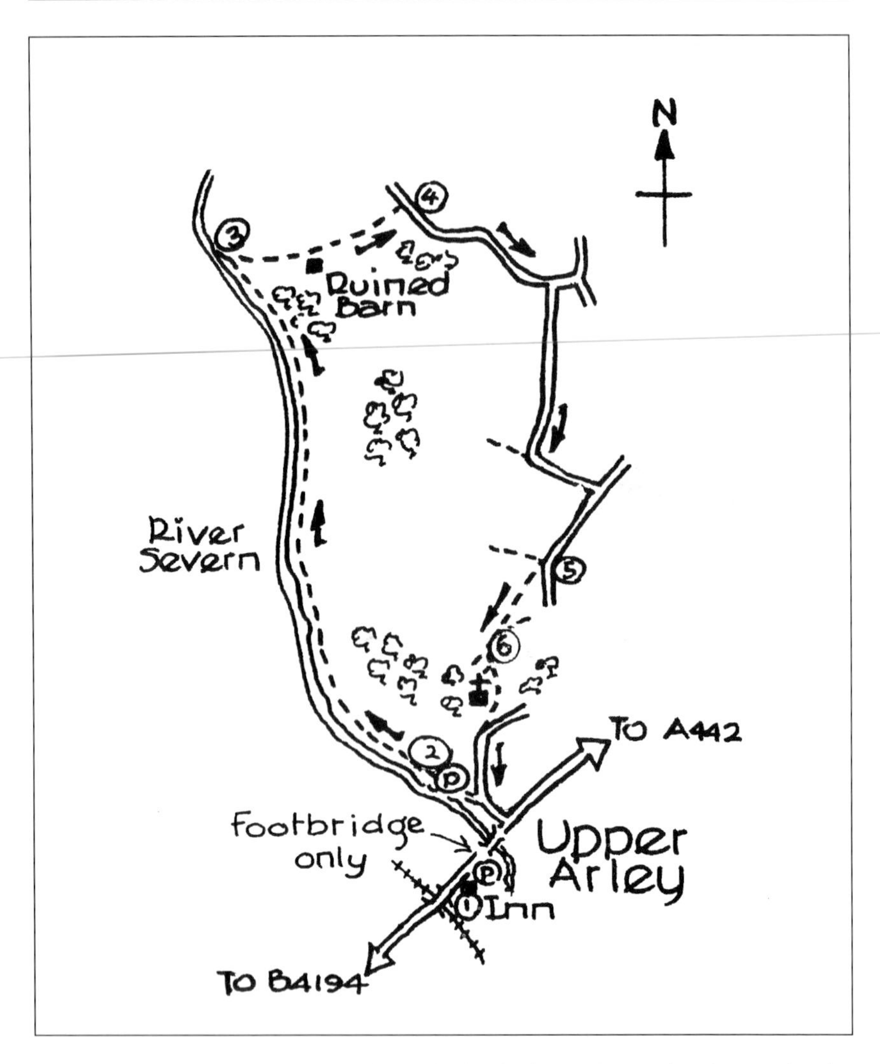

2. Walk through the car park and climb the stile at the far end. The path now hugs the riverbank, going through fields. After about 2 miles go through a wood to the pasture beyond. Stay by the river to the next stile but do not climb it.

3. Turn right to go through bushes; near the left-hand border of the meadow climb the ridge to a ruined farm building on the top. Keep ahead along the left-hand boundary to go through a metal gate. Maintain the direction to pass through another gate to a lane.

Steam on the Severn Valley Railway

4. Turn right. At a junction turn right. Within ¾ mile the lane bears left at another junction.

At a T-junction turn right. Within ⅓ mile take a signed path on the right by the drive to Bromley Farm.

5. Take the direction indicated on the finger post. Walk across the parkland then (maintaining the direction) pick up a vehicle drive.

6. Within a few steps there is a millstone directional sign (battlemented wall to right). Take the left-hand fork. At once the way divides again. Walk along the right fork – a narrower way – to a metal kissing gate. Keep ahead to pass through a wooden gate at the side of the 'Norman' gatehouse. Through another gate join a lane to return to Upper Arley. Retrace your steps over the river to the car park.

PLACES OF INTEREST NEARBY

The *Severn Valley Railway* runs for about 12 miles between Kidderminster and Bewdley. The route is often used by film and television companies – especially popular with the cameramen is the fine sight of trains passing over the cast-iron Victoria Bridge a mile south of Upper Arley. Trains run from March to the end of October. Telephone: 01299 403816. *Bridgnorth*, 10 miles north of Upper Arley, is a fascinating town as it is built on two levels joined by a cliff railway. In the top town is a castle wall – the only part of the fortification to have survived a violent Civil War battle.

WALK 2

WOLVERLEY: THE RIVER STOUR AND A 'STINKING DITCH'

Do not be put off by the title! The 'stinking ditch' is the Staffordshire and Worcester Canal, so called by the good folk of the inland port of Bewdley who disastrously thought they could thrive without Brindley's waterway (see Walk 4). It is a pleasant canal often cut through red sandstone and woodlands. This walk in the Stour valley crosses the river twice and includes a fascinating stretch on the canal towpath.

The Staffordshire and Worcester Canal

It was in 1772 that James Brindley, a brilliant Scottish engineer, opened his canal. It joined the River Severn where cargoes came up from the great ocean port of Bristol to the Trent and Mersey Canal, so giving commercial access to huge areas of the new industrial Midlands. The project (unlike so many hastily designed waterways) was a huge success paying high dividends to shareholders for many years.

Being a contour canal (and thus cutting down the number of locks)

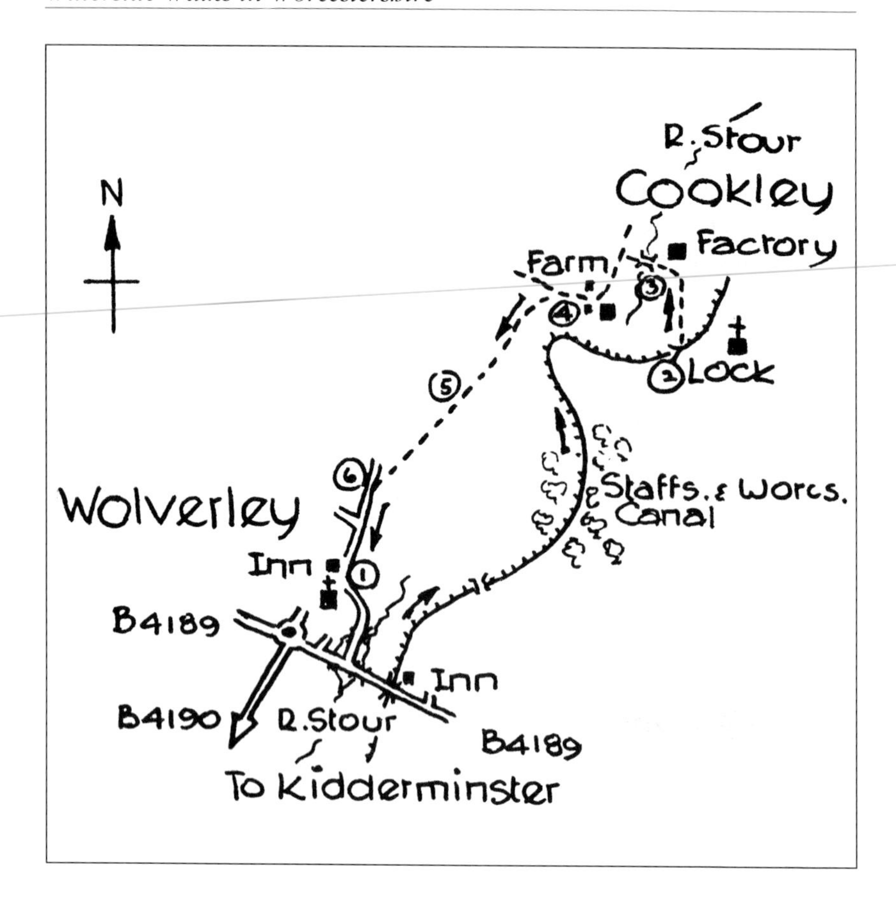

for much of its route the waterway follows the valley of the River Stour. A great advantage of this to walkers along the towpath today is that the vistas are continually changing with few tedious straight sections. It is also full of passing interest as (connecting with four other canals in its 46 miles) the canal is invariably busy.

The Stour is deceptive. It can look so placid but can also develop rapidly into a fast-flowing and even dangerous waterway. It is a common name for English rivers (there are at least half a dozen in the land) and in fact means 'strong and powerful'.

The walk is centred on the village of Wolverley with the old part clustered below steep red sandstone cliffs in which some homes were built. Sebright School was founded in Wolverley in 1620 and some magnificent buildings remain. Gazing down on the village from the clifftop is the church which was built in an exciting Italian style in the

18th century but was greatly altered by perhaps over-enthusiastic Victorian restorers about a hundred years ago.

Along the canal we reach Cookley. There is much new development here but in the 17th century there was a thriving ironworks which lasted for over a hundred years. Today there is a large factory which makes vehicle wheels.

There are several inns in Wolverley. The Lock is by the canal but is reached early on the walk. Returning into Wolverley village you come to the attractive Live and Let Live which offers 'the very best home cooked food'. The Queen's Head is conveniently situated in the main square and has a large car park and a beer garden. There is a pleasant restaurant which offers a good selection of food from Banks's pub menu. Particularly popular on chilly days are the casserole or the pork and ale sausages. The opening hours are 11.30 am to 2.30 pm and 5.30 pm to 11 pm on Monday to Friday with all day opening on Saturdays and Sundays. Telephone: 01563 850433.

- **HOW TO GET THERE:** Wolverley is on the B4189, 2 miles north of Kidderminster.

Some of the fine old buildings of Sebright School

- **PARKING:** There is some parking (limited) in the square at Wolverley. Alternatively, patrons may use the Queen's Head car park (obtain permission to leave your car while you walk).
- **LENGTH OF THE WALK:** 2½ miles. Map: OS Landranger 138 Kidderminster and Wyre Forest area (GR 830793).

THE WALK

1. From the square walk along the road with the clifftop church on the right. Cross the River Stour to the B4189 and turn left. By the inn gain the canal towing path. Turn left. The attractive waterway runs alongside steep cliffs and overlooks the river valley.

2. At a lock and bridge leave the canal by climbing a stile to a pasture left. Cut across the field towards a factory. We reach the canal again at a stile. Do not climb this but turn left to walk alongside a right-hand brick wall.

3. Keep by the wall through gates or over a stile. Again cross over the River Stour. Continue along a rough vehicle way. At a T-junction of tracks turn left then bear right by a house. Keep ahead with a barn on the right and an old timber barn on the left.

4. At a waymark post keep to the track just to the left of the post to a gate by a pond. Two paths are signed here. Take the left-hand way to maintain the direction over the hill. On the top of the rise bear left to pick up the side of a wood and a wire fence to a corner stile. The path is clear beyond but watch out for stinging nettles!

5. In a field keep by the left-hand border to join a tractor way. Maintain the heading to arrive at a road.

6. Turn left to Wolverley.

PLACES OF INTEREST NEARBY

Ten miles to the north-east (through Stourbridge and Brierly Hill) is Dudley and the *Black Country Museum*. The museum has a fascinating range of live and 'hands-on' exhibits tracing the industrial past of the region. Open daily. Telephone: 0121 557 9643.

WALK 3

THE BITTELL RESERVOIRS

The willow-fringed reservoirs built to supply the Worcester and Birmingham Canal are fed from many streams tumbling off the Lickey Hills and now provide a fine resource for yachtsmen, anglers, birdlife and, of course, walkers. After a stretch of the canal towpath this varied waterside walk leads you beside and between all three reservoirs.

Upper Bittell Reservoir

The difficulty of constructing the Worcester and Birmingham Canal so that it could take craft to the top of the 400 foot Birmingham plateau was obtaining an adequate water supply. Further downhill a unique lift designed by John Woodhouse was considered and installed experimentally at Tardebigge and opened in 1811. After a cloudburst the lift was damaged and abandoned in favour of locks (see Walk 7).

This increased the water problem; it was initially solved by pumping water from 100 foot deep wells and the pumps were used for almost a hundred years until 1914 but they had in fact become largely redundant when vast reservoirs were built on the borders of

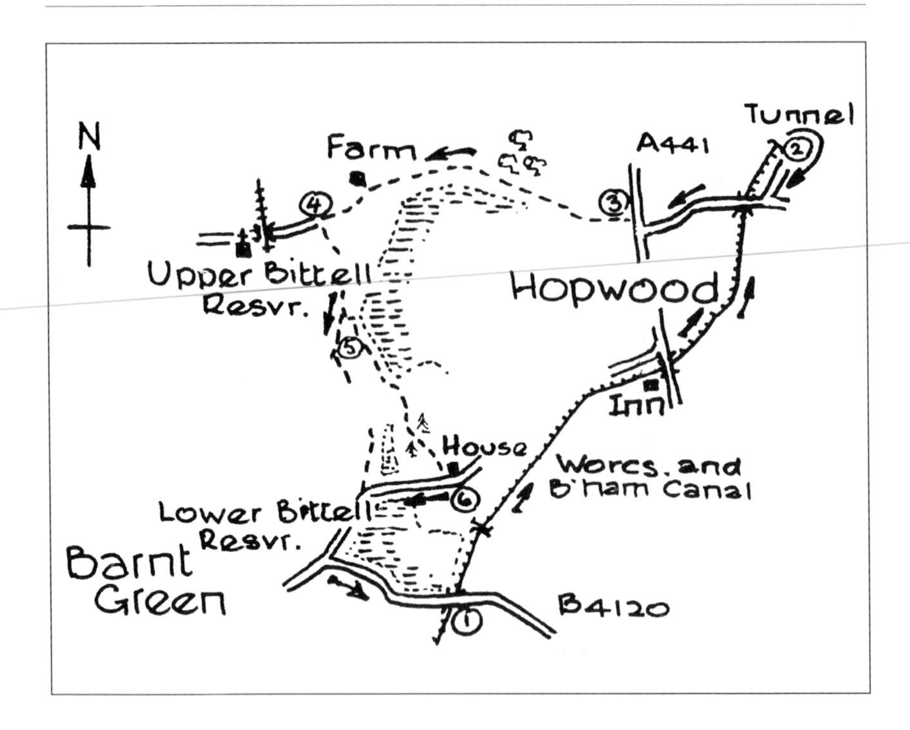

Birmingham in 1832 almost twenty years after the canal was opened.

On this reservoir and canal walk we pass near a fine little church which is cosseted in trees at Cofton Hackett. The pinnacled bellcote is 15th century. Not far away is the Hall which conceals what is said by Pevsner to be 'one of the finest late medieval halls in Worcestershire'; the Hall was another refuge of King Charles I in 1645 during his flight from the Parliamentarians.

The inn on the route is prettily situated alongside the canal. The Hopwood House Inn is one of the Milestone Taverns which have a good reputation for food in pleasant surroundings. There is a fine children's playground and a large grassed area. The full range of Banks's beers is offered and especially good value is the Lunch'n Early two course menu. The inn is open all day. Telephone: 0121 351 1388.

- **HOW TO GET THERE:** The starting point is almost a mile east of Barnt Green along the B4120.
- **PARKING:** There is limited off-road parking near the canal bridge.
- **LENGTH OF THE WALK:** 5 miles. Map: OS Landranger 139 Birmingham and Wolverhampton (GR 020739).

The Walk

1. From the road gain the towing path and walk with the water on the left side. Lower Bittell Reservoir is also to the left. Keeping to the waterway go under bridges, passing the canalside inn at Hopwood. We reach the entrance to the Wast Hill Tunnel (almost one and a half miles long).

2. Climb the steps to Wast Hill Lane and turn right to a junction. Turn right (signed to Hopwood).

3. At the main road cross and turn right then at once left down a vehicle drive which is signed as a footpath. At the end go through a kissing gate and take the signed direction to walk the length of the pasture.

Climb a far stile and follow the track ahead. To the left is a muddy area which is the fringe of another reservoir – it is an SSSI – a Site of Special Scientific Interest. At a waymark post is a junction of paths. Keep ahead along a clear path which borders fields and passes a farm. Walk along the drive.

The old pumphouse of the Upper Bittell Reservoir

4. At the start of a lane turn left. (Cofton Hackett church and the Hall are further along the lane, beyond the railway). We pass attractive pools where swans glide. At the end of the pools climb a stile on the left. Pass a solid stone pump house to reach the dam of Upper Bittell Reservoir.

5. Turn right along the embankment. At the end go over a step stile. Take the arrowed direction over a knoll topped with firs. Follow the clear path which keeps at the edges of fields then goes to the right of a house to a stile to a lane.

6. Turn right. The lane passes between two reservoirs – a good viewing point for waterfowl. At a junction turn left along the B4120 to the start.

Places of Interest Nearby

Five miles north of Barnt Green and well signed along the A38 is *Cadbury World.* This is the place for chocoholics; it traces the history of Cadburys and chocolate in fascinating displays and of course there is the inevitable shop to taste the products! Open daily. Telephone: 0121 451 4159.

WALK 4

BEWDLEY: AN AMBLE ALONG TWO WATERWAYS

There is a contrast between the two waterways we walk beside on this route: the Severn is the mightiest of Britain's rivers; Dowles Brook is a small tributary twisting this way and that to take us into the heart of the Wyre Forest – and occasionally, if we're very lucky, allowing us a glimpse of the elusive kingfisher.

The waterfront at Bewdley

Dowles Brook, which joins the Severn north of Bewdley, was loved by the author Francis Brett Young; in his evocative book *Far Forest* he mentions the stream and Gladden Brook. He called the Wyre Forest 'Werewood' and like the real thing his description of 'a confusion of tumbled hills and villages, mysterious and secret and lost to the outer world as any in western England' is very apposite.

Before the notorious Beeching axe fell there was a picturesque railway which chased Dowles Brook upstream. It crossed the Severn

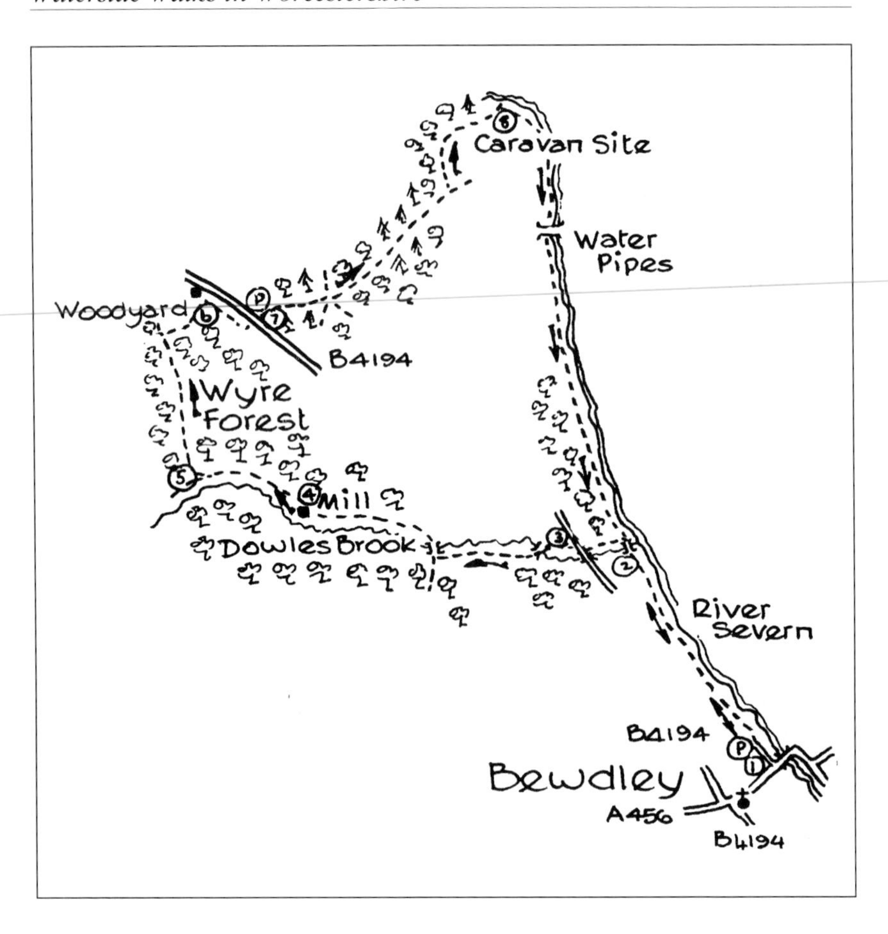

over high stanchions. The bridge has long gone but the pillars remain like guardians of the country scene.

The story is told of a lady passenger admiring the honeysuckle which overhung the tracks; the guard stopped the train and picked a bunch of the fragrant flowers to present to her. Such was the England of yesteryear!

The start of this walk is at Bewdley. Perhaps the name has origins in the French 'Beaulieu' or it was a 'ley' or forest clearing. The traveller Leland many centuries ago said that 'the whole towne glittereth being all new buildings'; Pevsner said it was 'the most perfect small Georgian town in Worcestershire'; a guidebook went even further by naming Bewdley one of the most beautiful towns in England! So it is well worth a perambulation before the walk proper!

Bewdley was once a bustling inland port and the warehouses on the quay remind us that the special flat-bottomed boats called trows conveyed the cargoes from Bristol. When James Brindley wanted to bring the Staffordshire and Worcester Canal to the town he was told that Bewdley did not want the 'stinking ditch'. The new town of Stourport downstream therefore was created and prospered and Bewdley never recovered.

The river is crossed by the three-arched bridge built by Telford in 1801. Outside the town is Tickenhill Palace; it was here in 1499 that the young Prince Arthur of Wales was married by proxy to Catherine of Aragon.

There are many pubs and eating places in Bewdley; some are by the river where you can watch the world (and the pleasure craft) go by as you dine. The Mug House just north of the river bridge is ideally situated on the quayside. It offers a modest but reasonably priced bill of fare (try the Balti on a winter's day!) and a wide range of Banks's beers. The pub is open all day. Telephone: 01299 404740.

The mill on Dowles Brook in the Wyre Forest

- **HOW TO GET THERE:** Bewdley is 20 miles west of Birmingham along the A456.
- **PARKING:** There are signed car parks in Bewdley; alternatively, leave your car at the Forest Centre car park on the B4194 for a shorter walk (starting at point 7).
- **LENGTH OF THE WALK:** 5½ miles. Map: OS Landranger 138 Kidderminster and Wyre Forest area (GR 788754).

THE WALK

1. By Telford's fine bridge at Bewdley walk along the road with the river to the right. Keep ahead to go by seats and a garden. After about a mile of waterside walking cross over a bridge across Dowles Brook.

2. At once turn left along a rough vehicle track to a road. Turn right. Just past the place where the railway bridge once was cross the road and continue along a path into the woods.

3. Soon the tumbling Dowles Brook emerges from under the old railway embankment. Follow the waters downstream to a vehicle way. Turn right. When the track divides take the right-hand way and cross the brook.

Pass a reserve administered by the Worcestershire Nature Conservation Trust then Knowles Mill – an idyllic spot with the mill-keeper's cottage alongside.

4. Keep along the main track to enter (through a gate) the Wyre Forest National Nature Reserve – one of Britain's largest ancient oak woodlands. Continue for 200 yards.

5. Turn sharp right along a path signed by a yellow arrow. Keep on the main forest road at all junctions (now following red ringed posts). A woodyard is reached then a stile to a nearby road.

6. Do not climb the stile but take a path right. This leads after 300 yards to another stile to the road. Cross to the Hawkbatch car park and picnic place. Follow the vehicle way to the end.

7. By the information board take the path between two wooden posts. Keep ahead to pass a post of multi-coloured rings. Turn right at a T-junction of tracks.

Through a barrier take a path almost straight across by a green ringed post. The track drops down to a junction of several ways (notice the sword wood carving nearby). Keep ahead along a wide way. Just before the end of the woods take a signed path left (private road but public path). The 'road' bends around a secluded caravan park to drop down to a 'Private Woodlands' notice. Here the signed path goes off to the right to drop sharply down to the river.

8. Turn right along the riverside path. The path goes under a fine cast-iron bridge that carries Birmingham's water supply from North Wales (downhill all the way without the need of pumps!). The path passes the giant old railway bridge stanchions then rejoins the outward route to return to Bewdley.

Places of Interest Nearby

West Midlands Safari Park is between Bewdley and Kidderminister. It is unashamedly a place of fun. Besides the free-roam animals which you view from your car (monkeys have a tendency to cadge a lift on the top) there are many amusements, animal shows and refreshment places etc. The park is open daily. Telephone: 01562 777267.

WALK 5

BELBROUGHTON AND A BUSY LITTLE BROOK

This walk follows the lovely brooks which created the power to drive labour-intensive local industry – the world-famous manufacture of scythes. This was an essential tool for countrymen for many centuries.

The brook at Drayton that powered the mill

How dependent were industrialists in the past on an adequate water supply from brooks to power their machinery. Many brooks tumbled down from the high lands of the Lickey Hills on the outskirts of Birmingham and through the villages of Bell and Broughton (which united to become Belbroughton). Here (Broughton means 'village on the brook') many mills were built using water over and over again in each succeeding mill along the water-course.

Many of the mills were to manufacture scythes and swords but others were for making carpets and grinding corn. There are fine signs on entering the village, immediately reminding us of the importance of

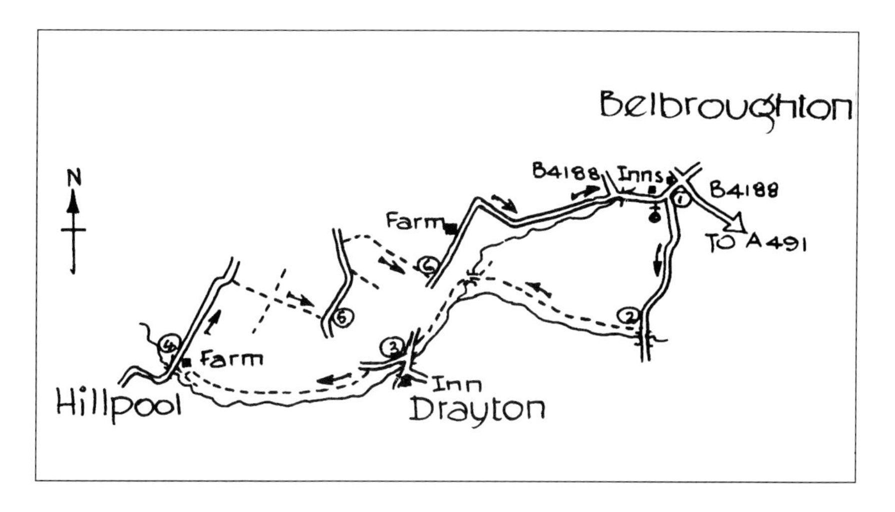

the scythe industry. It lasted for well over a century and employed over a hundred workers at its peak until the last works closed in 1968.

Sadly the scythe, hay knives and billhooks are no longer required in this mechanised age but the products of the many mills owned by Isaac Nash were world famous in their day. Latterly electricity powered the machinery rather than the waters of Belne Brook and it was said that automation could not tackle the jobs economically; unfortunately this proved not to be true.

Some of the old mill buildings remain and (together with the millpools) can be seen on the walk when the paths border the brooks. Now Belbroughton is mainly a commuter village with the inhabitants travelling to work elsewhere. Belbroughton once supported eleven inns but only four remain today.

The Talbot makes a special point of attracting families, with a separate menu containing all the old favourites for children. There is a good selection of beer including Banks's. Telephone: 01562 730249. Along the route is the Robin Hood at the hamlet of Drayton (the name was given when the Ancient Order of Foresters expanded in the last century). Again children are welcomed here with a rather good adventure playground and plenty of grassed areas. The beers include Bass and Burton and there is draught Gaymer's cider. There are traditional meals but more unusual dishes are listed on the 'specials' board. It is open 12 noon to 2.30 pm and 6.30 pm to 11 pm Monday to Saturday. Normal hours are kept on Sunday. Telephone: 01562 730255.

The 18th-century Drayton House overlooks the mill pool

- **HOW TO GET THERE:** Belbroughton lies on the B4188 which runs between the A491 and the A450 south of Hagley.
- **PARKING:** Quiet streetside off the main road.
- **LENGTH OF THE WALK:** 4 miles. Map: OS Landranger 139 Birmingham and Wolverhampton (GR 920771).

THE WALK

1. From the centre of the village walk along Church Road and pass the church on the right (note the memorial to Nash – the scythe-maker – by the gate). Within ⅓ mile and just before a house gateway (on the left) go over a stile on the right.

2. Walk along a farm track with a brook on the left. Go over a stile by a gate to rough grassland. At a signed junction of paths take the right-hand path. Continue alongside a right-hand boundary to a far stile. Over this proceed along a wooded fenced way to a vehicle way. Turn left along a rough track which then bears right.

Here leave the main track to continue along a path which borders another brook (on the right). The path runs alongside a left-hand brick wall. Go over a railed bridge to cross the brook. Immediately regain the old heading but with the brook now on the left side. Climb a corner stile and stay by the brook and pools to a stile onto a lane at Drayton. Turn left.

3. Pass former mill buildings then (just before the road goes over the brook) turn right along a lane signed to Hillpool. Just past houses take a path over a stile left. The brook again is on the left. Walk at the borders of fields.

Farm buildings are neared. Climb a corner stile then another to turn left to a vehicle way. Turn right to a lane at Hillpool. The brook rushes underneath here.

4. Turn right along the lane, which has been cut through the red sandstone. After 400 yards take a signed path on the right. Walk directly away from the lane alongside a right-hand hedge. In a corner go through a wide hedge gap and keep ahead over the open field to the opposite hedge. Climb a stile and maintain the heading over another open field to a stile on the crown of the hill.

5. Turn left on the lane. Go past a signed path. A few steps further take a signed bridleway on the right. Follow the hedged way to a lane.

6. Turn left and follow the lane to Belbroughton, passing more old mill pools.

Places of Interest Nearby

Five miles along lanes south-west of Belbroughton is *Harvington Hall* which is renowned for the number and ingenuity of its priests' hiding holes. The Hall is open daily and there is a restaurant. Telephone: 01562 777267.

WALK 6

WHITHER? BY WATER TO WITHYBED!

The Worcester and Birmingham Canal provides the water on this walk. The area is surprisingly attractive and rural considering it is not many miles from the city of Birmingham.

The Worcester and Birmingham Canal

Cruises by canal boats are now very popular with holidaymakers eager to escape from the hustle and bustle of everyday life. Instead of the maelstrom of a motorway there is a boat chugging along to cover just a mile or so in the hour. Many of these cruises start from Withybed Green near Alvechurch where there is a large boatyard and marina.

The canal is the Worcester and Birmingham which is 30 miles in length but not without some work as there is an average of one lock for every two miles of waterway. Holidaymakers love to cover a circle using the canal to Birmingham then meandering along the Stratford-on-Avon Canal. The River Avon navigation goes to the Severn and the return is along the original canal from Worcester using the spectacular Tardebigge flight.

Alvechurch has some attractive buildings although they are somewhat overwhelmed by the rapid expansion of the village over recent years. The place was named after Aelfgyth – a lady who founded a church in AD 780. It was on the site of the present church of St Laurence which has Norman and Saxon work. However, the building rather suffered at the hands of perhaps over-enthusiastic Victorian 'restorers'; they literally 'raised the roof' which does take some of the beauty away from the Norman tower.

Alvechurch was once the summer retreat of the Bishops of Worcester. The palace was described by the chronicler Leland as 'the byshope of Wircester's fayr manor place'. Nothing remains of the splendour today except some hillocks and the outlines of a moat.

The inn on the route is the Crown Inn – picturesquely sited alongside the canal at Withybed Green. (No doubt it was hereabouts that many willows were grown for making into baskets.) The inn is always flower-bedecked in summertime – and there is always a bowl of water for my spaniel companion Cass while I enjoy the Mitchell and Butler's beer with baguettes filled with meats and salads! The early 19th century inn once depended on the canal trade as it was a resting place for the bargees and horses. Nowadays the pub is open daily from 11 am to 2.30 pm and 7 pm to 11 pm on Monday to Saturday with normal Sunday hours applying. Telephone: 0121 445 2300.

- **HOW TO GET THERE:** Turn westwards off the A441, 3 miles north of Redditch, signed Cobley Hill. The canal is reached after 1 mile.
- **PARKING:** There is roadside parking near the canal bridge (limited) – or you could start at the public car park at Withybed Green, picking up the walk in point 3.
- **LENGTH OF THE WALK:** 3½ miles. Map: OS Landranger 139 Birmingham and Wolverhampton (GR 020712).

The Walk

1. From the road gain the towing path and walk with the water on your left side. The waterway twists this way and that so the views are constantly changing. Go past bridge 60. At the next (numbered 61) is the Crown Inn. At bridge 64 leave the canal.

2. Gain the road and turn left to cross the water. Follow the road under the railway and past a road junction. A hundred yards beyond take a signed bridleway through a gate left.

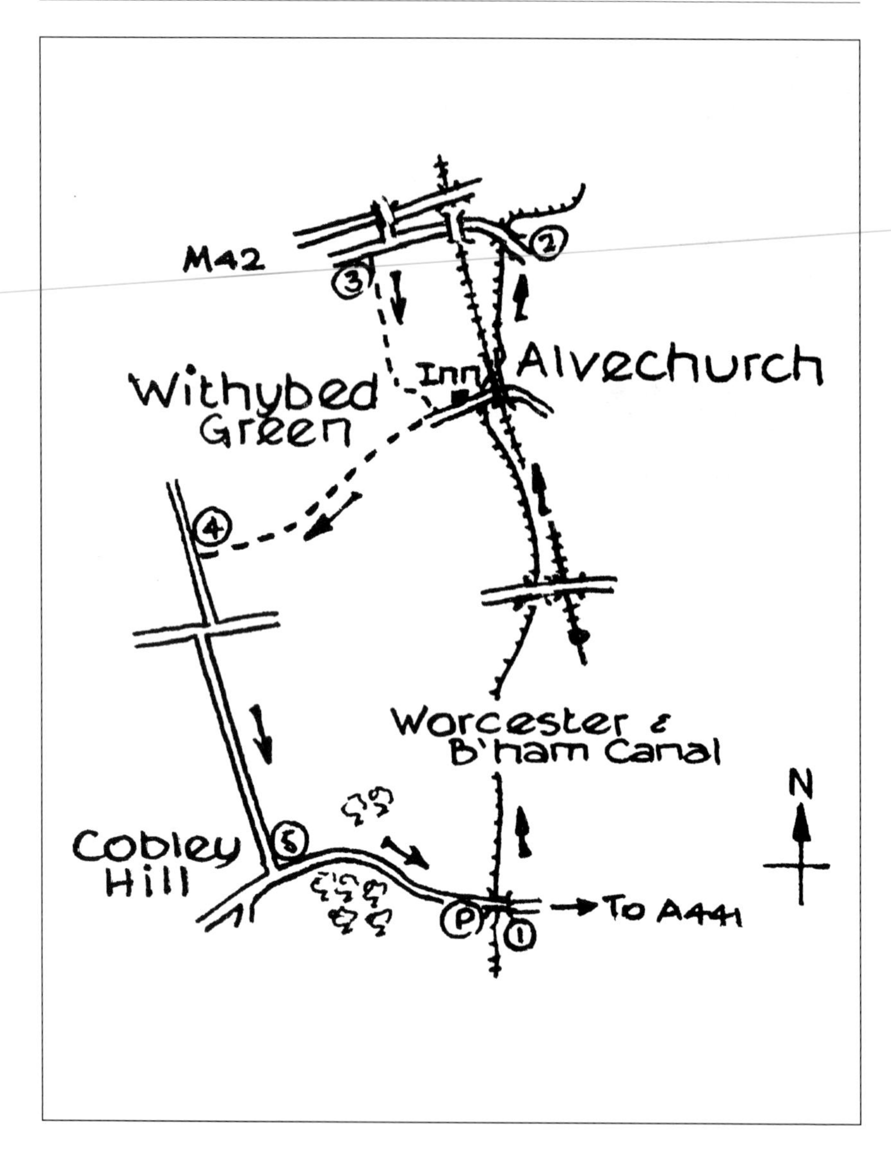

3. The bridleway is well used beside a wall and becomes Birches Lane. At a T-junction turn right to walk in front of cottages. Go over a stile to a pasture. Walk uphill by a left-hand border. Climb another stile. There is a waymark arrow but note the route is rather to the right of the indicated direction. We go through a gateway (no gate). Continue climbing to a stile by barn conversions and then to a lane.

The canal bridge at Alvechurch

4. Turn left. At a T-junction go right then immediately left (Cobley Hill).

5. At the next junction turn left to drop down to the canal bridge.

Places of Interest Nearby

The Midland Bus and Transport Museum is at Wythall – about 3 miles along lanes north-east of Alvechurch. This has a wonderful collection of vehicles that evokes many memories of days past. It is open at weekends from 9 am to 7 pm. Telephone: 01564 826471.

WALK 7

TARDEBIGGE: AMBLING BESIDE A WONDER OF BRITAIN!

...again the Worcester and Birmingham Canal. The series of waterway locks on the Tardebigge Flight is quite hard work for holidaymakers and the 'captains' and crews often welcome a helping hand from the towpath walker!

Tardebigge top lock

The deep lock at Tardebigge (the deepest in the land) has been described as a 'wonder of Britain'. Birmingham and the vast array of industries of the Black Country are on a high plateau which created a problem for the builders of the canals which were the arteries of trade. With the Worcestershire and Birmingham Canal the engineers found the solution to lifting craft 400 feet by building a long flight of locks (with the extra deep top lock) and several long tunnels.

This waterway was very expensive with so many locks (58 in a distance of only 15 miles). The inland sailors on the Tardebigge Flight which we walk alongside on this walk have to negotiate 30 locks within 2½ miles – which sounds like hard holiday work!

Before the famous top lock was constructed the intention was to use a vertical lift operated by chains and pulleys. The tests when over 100 boats were raised in 12 hours were considered a success but then disaster struck. There was a local cloudburst and the lift was severely damaged; the go-ahead was given for the Tardebigge Flight to be built instead.

A further problem now was the provision of so much water for the locks. There was often a water shortage; it was solved at first by pumping water from a 100 foot well but later several large reservoirs were built.

The whole length of the canal with all the difficulties of the terrain was finally opened in 1815. Two pubs were provided at Tardebigge especially for the workers but neither now remain.

From a lofty height a church with a beautiful slender spire overlooks the canal. There was once a 12th century Norman church on the site but this was pulled down in the 18th century and the present structure (often called 'a Georgian masterpiece') was completed. Inside there are memorials to the Archer family. They were the Earls of Plymouth and lived at nearby Hewell Grange from 1542. Today the mansion is run by the prison service!

The Tardebigge Inn is near the start on the B4096, in a fine building with a tower. It was once the village hall and provided by the benevolent Archer family in 1911. There were many activities here both educational and leisure. A bath could be enjoyed for a penny! However when the family lost Hewell Grange and the estate was sold off the village lost its hall (and its baths!) and gained a pub. This still provides much pleasure for children as there is an amusement hut and plenty of space. Families are made welcome and the place (specialising in steaks) is open all day. Telephone: 01527 550050.

- **HOW TO GET THERE:** The walk starts by Tardebigge church which is off the B4096, 3 miles north-west of Redditch.
- **PARKING:** There is a car park near the church.
- **LENGTH OF THE WALK:** 5 miles. Map: OS Landranger 139 Birmingham and Wolverhampton, with a short section on 150 Worcester and The Malverns (GR 997691).

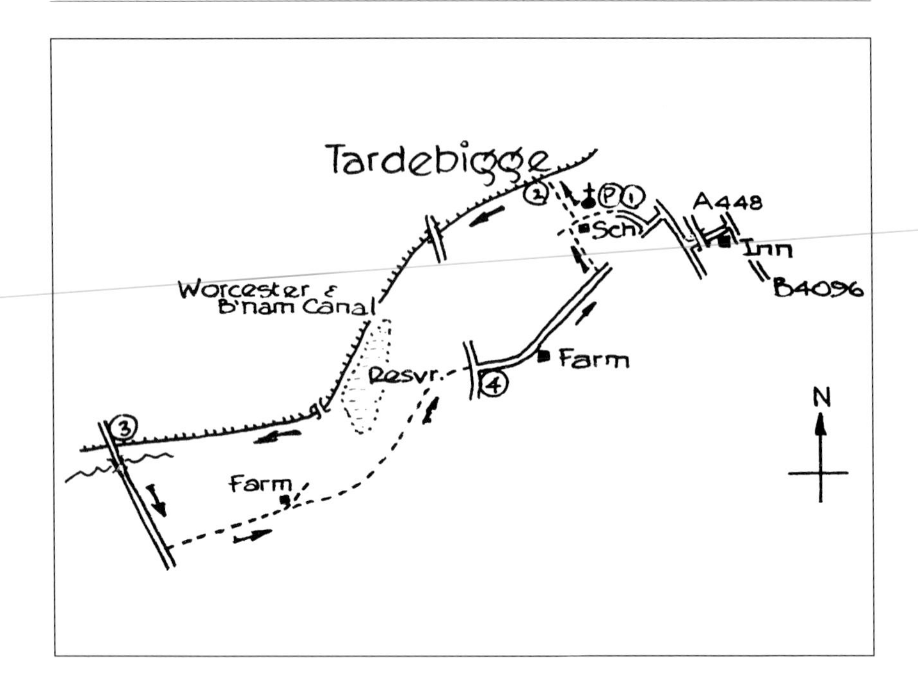

The Walk

1. Pass through the kissing gate by the car park and into the churchyard of Tardebigge church. Walk along the path to the left of the church with the school (which some say was once a pub!) on the left. Just past the church and footpath sign turn 90 degrees right to walk along a paved path. Go past a seat (fine viewpoint) to drop down to a corner stile. In the pasture keep descending to climb a stile to the canal just to the right of the lock-keeper's cottage.

2. Here is that deep top lock of the celebrated Tardebigge Flight. There is also a seat that reminds us that it was here Tom Rolt met Robert Aickman on his boat *Cressy* to form the Inland Waterways Association in 1946. Turn left along the towing path with the water on your right. Follow the waterway for about 2 miles, passing (on the left) a large 'topping up' reservoir.

3. Leave the canal at bridge 51 and lock 41. Gain the road and turn left. Within ⅓ mile turn left. The footpath is signed down a farm drive. At the farm keep to the right of the buildings to pick up a bridleway which you follow to a lane at a junction of ways.

The lovely spire of Tardebigge church

4. Cross to High House Lane. Follow the lane around bends to a signed path over a stile left. In a playing field follow the left-hand border then a fenced way to the churchyard. Turn right and retrace your steps to the car park.

Places of Interest Nearby

Avoncroft Museum of Buildings, about 3 miles west of Tardebigge, contains a wonderful assortment of domestic, town and agricultural buildings that have been removed from Midland sites and skilfully reconstructed, including the Danzey Green windmill where the sails turn again to grind corn for flour which is sold. There are picnic tables and restaurant facilities. Open daily in summer; varied hours in winter. Telephone for details: 01527 831363. *Bordesley Abbey ruins* are on the northern outskirts of Redditch. There is an exhibition site which is open daily during the summer. Ring first for winter opening hours. Nearby (same admission) is the *Forge Mill Needle Museum* which traces the history of the industry in the town. Telephone: 01527 62509.

WALK 8

POETIC WATERSIDE STEPS NEAR DODFORD

Many brooks tumble off the heights of the Lickey Hills; some are given a name but are of little beauty; others are un-named but are anything but nondescript. The brook experienced on this walk is of the latter kind and never fails to give delight. The poet A.E. Housman, whose birthplace we pass, loved this area too. From the gentle uplands above the valley he must have gazed far into the Welsh borderlands and 'those blue remember'd hills' and sought out that 'loveliest of trees, the cherry'.

The Dodford Inn is reached from a path by the brook

The little village of Dodford is an interesting place. Looking at the map it will be seen that the streets are laid out in straight lines – so unlike the typical haphazard patterns in most English villages.

It was in the middle of the last century that Fergus O'Connor had the visionary scheme to establish a Chartist village. Each settler from the towns and cities was given a four-acre plot on which to create a

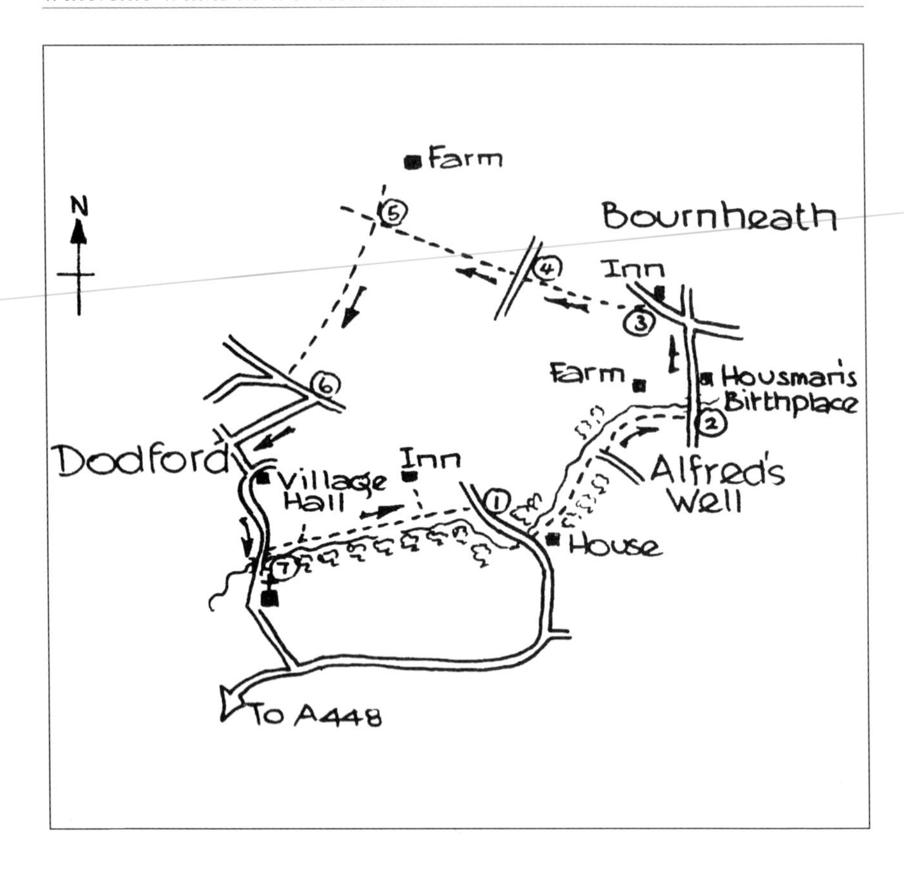

self sufficient smallholding. Sadly, settlers had little knowledge of agricultural practices; the soil was clay and heavy and difficult to work. However, the Chartists turned to strawberry growing which was more suited to the conditions until a virus took hold and ruined the crops.

There is a plaque commemorating the Dodford Chartists outside the modern village hall. This was once the site of the church but in 1908 a new building ½ mile away was constructed, said by Pevsner to be 'the best church of its date in the county'. Not far away are the few remains of a priory which was founded in 1184 for Augustinian canons.

Just off the route is the Dodford Inn with a path alongside which dips down to our brook. This is a Greenalls house which has been tastefully modernised but offers mainly traditional food. Outside there are plenty of grassed areas for children's play and a caravan site. Flexible opening hours apply at this welcoming pub. Telephone: 01527 832470.

- **HOW TO GET THERE:** Turn north off the A448 – signed for Dodford – 2 miles west of Bromsgrove. Do not turn left to Dodford but keep ahead at two junctions to drop steeply down to the brook.
- **PARKING:** There is a small parking area by the brook.
- **LENGTH OF THE WALK:** 3½ miles. Map: OS Landranger 139 Birmingham and Wolverhampton (GR 942727).

THE WALK

1. Walk south along the lane for 300 yards. By a white house turn left along a signed path. Follow a lovely track through the trees to climb a stile to a meadow. Keep ahead by the right-hand boundary to another stile. Descend steps then bear right to drop down to a lane.

Walk along the lane a few steps then take a signed path over a stile left. Continue along a well-used track through woods high above the stream. Climb a stile to a large pasture. Bear left to pass an isolated tree then walk to the left of stables. Continue to a lane.

The birthplace of the poet, A. E. Housman

2. Turn left to pass Housman's birthplace (not open to the public). At a crossroads turn left (signed for Belbroughton). Little houses are passed – these were nailers' residences when this was a cottage industry. You come to a pub.

3. On a bend take the signed path on the left. Climb a stile and walk beside a holly hedge then go over a corner stile. In a large meadow bear right and follow a right-hand border to a stile on a ridge by trees. Again follow a right-hand border to drop down to a double step stile by a gate. Climb a hill (left-hand hedge) to a stile to a lane.

4. Cross to the opposite path. In a horse jump field walk at the edge to climb a corner stile then another by a gateway (no gate). The next stile can now be seen in the opposite boundary. Take the arrowed direction to drop down to a stile. Maintain the heading (left-hand hedge) to a corner stile onto a bridleway.

5. Turn left. Follow the bridleway to a lane at Dodford. Turn left and continue to Victoria Road.

6. Turn right here and at a crossroads turn left to a T-junction by the village hall. Turn right. Within ⅓ mile turn left.

7. The bridleway is signed down a vehicle way. As this swings left to a house take the signed path right. The path soon joins the brook. Follow this – the path to the Dodford Inn goes off to the left – to reach the lane and the parking place.

Places of Interest Nearby

In this Housman countryside it is interesting to visit other places associated with the great poet. Besides his birthplace, passed on the walk, he spent many happy years early in his life at *Perry Hall* (now an hotel) on the A448 just out of Bromsgrove. Not far from the birthplace is a plaque on a wall stating that another home now demolished (The Clock House) stood near. To the north is the village of *Catshill.* Housman's grandfather was the parson here.

WALK 9

SHRAWLEY WOOD AND ASTLEY: DAWDLING BESIDE DICK BROOK

The waters of Dick Brook meander a twisting way through a lovely wooded valley before being swallowed by the mighty Severn. The village we visit on this walk – Astley – produced one of the longest serving prime ministers between the wars – Sir Stanley Baldwin.

Checking the route at Dick Brook

Dick Brook is now a tranquil stream but the height of the banks gives a clue that this could well have been the first canalised brook in England. Craft would use the water to convey raw materials and iron between the ironworks and the important commercial route of the River Severn.

Nothing remains to indicate the extent of the canal and documentary facts are very sparse. We can see the present extent of the woodlands which once were all administered by the Shrawley Wood House Estate (now many acres are in the hands of Forest Enterprise –

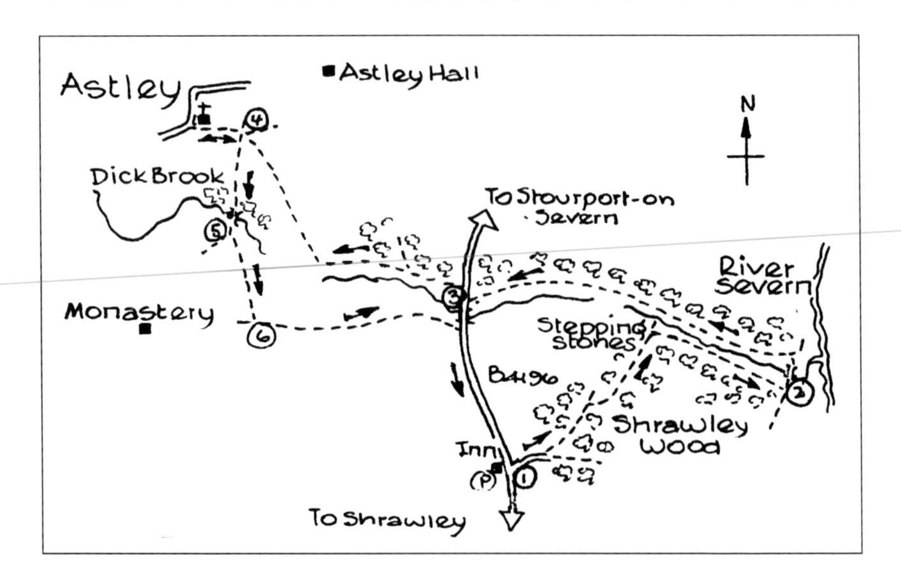

the former Forestry Commission). However, it is known that many trees were felled to fuel the fires of the ironworks and potteries.

The locals are also proud of the fact that Shrawley oaks were used to repair the Houses of Parliament after bomb damage during the Second World War. There are also vast tracts of lime trees which – now scarce – were in Saxon times the dominant trees in most forests of England and Wales. This has led to Shrawley Wood being designated a SSSI – a Site of Special Scientific Interest.

The route climbs out of the valley of Dick Brook to the little village of Astley. The hilltop church here has much work of the Norman masons to admire. In the churchyard is the grave of W H Havergal. He was minister here for 20 years in the early 19th century and a noted composer of his day. However, his daughter, who was born in the rectory, is better known today – Frances Ridley wrote the words of many popular hymns.

On the nearby B4196 road is a memorial to Astley's most famous son. The stone is inscribed 'At the top of this hill in Astley Hall lived and died Stanley Baldwin 1867-1947 – three times Prime Minister'.

The New Inn is by the car park at the start of the walk. This is a friendly Marston's pub which specialises in home cooking. Telephone: 01299 822701. Off the route, just ⅓ mile along the road (south) to Shrawley, is the Rose and Crown (Banks's beer) which actively welcomes ramblers with its invitation to 'Walk in Shrawley Wood from here'. I called on a chilly day and the liver and bacon in an onion gravy was just right at the end of the walk. The pub is open at lunchtime and in the evenings on Monday to Friday but is open all day on Saturday and Sunday. Telephone: 01905 620410.

Also by the start is the village Post Office and Stores which sells food for a picnic.

- **HOW TO GET THERE:** Shrawley is 5 miles south of Stourport-on-Severn along the B4196.
- **PARKING:** There is a free public car park and picnic place behind the New Inn.
- **LENGTH OF THE WALK:** 4 miles. Map: OS Landranger 138 Kidderminster and Wyre Forest area (GR 799663).

THE WALK

1. Opposite the New Inn and by the shop take the lane signed as a no through road. The lane becomes a vehicle way through a gate to Shrawley Wood. At once there are two tracks. Take the left-hand way to pass the information board.

Climb a rise. Within 300 yards and just past a red ringed post you come to a junction of ways (the waymarking post was down on my survey visit). Turn right and stay on the main track, passing another red ringed post. Follow the clear path which descends to a vale which is a delight with foxgloves in early summer.

We reach Dick Brook by a lovely spot with stepping stones. Do not cross the water but stay on the track with the stream now on the left side.

2. At a bridge, turn left to cross Dick Brook to a pasture. There are two stiles ahead; climb the left-hand one to a bold track. Turn left along a way never far from the stream to the main road.

3. Go right a few steps then cross the road to a signed bridleway. Go through a gate by a cottage and keep ahead to walk by the brook and through woods. After a few hundred yards there is a division of ways. Leave the bridleway to take the footpath signed (yellow arrow) off to the left.

Out of the wood climb a fence stile. Bear right over rough ground where there is no clear path as you climb to a hedge gap (or gate) to a huge arable field. Aim just to the right of the distant church over the open field. Continue to a stile and gate.

Astley Church

4. Over the stile follow the arrowed way ahead which leads to Astley and the church. (Stanley Baldwin's Astley Hall – now a nursing home – is to the right.)

Retrace your steps to the gate and stile. Do not climb the stile but turn right to descend again to the valley of Dick Brook. Go past a waymark post to a Y-junction of ways. Take the right-hand fork to cross the stream to a crossroads of tracks.

5. Turn left through the gate. Follow the bold path through the trees and fields. Away to the right you will glimpse Glasshampton Monastery which was established in 1918 as a noviciate of St Francis of Cerne Abbas. Continue to a wide vehicle track.

6. Turn left to the B4196. Turn right to the New Inn and the car park.

Places of Interest Nearby

Stourport-on-Severn, to the north, developed when Brindley joined the Severn with his Staffordshire and Worcester Canal here and created an important inland commercial port. Today it is a place for day trippers to come for fun. There are amusements, riverside inns and plenty of river trips and activities. *Astley Vineyard* (which is signposted from the B4196 a mile north of Dick Brook) has gained a great reputation for the quality of its English wines. Here you can taste and buy! Telephone: 01299 822907.

WALK 10

HANBURY: A CANAL AND ANCIENT FOREST WALK

The Worcester and Birmingham canal runs alongside a great railway route from the Midlands to the south-west so now and then the peace of the countryside hereabouts is disturbed by the thunder of trains. However, nothing except birdsong disturbs the tranquil wood on Piper's Hill, passed on our route.

The canal near Hanbury

The Worcester and Birmingham Canal was cut by the navvies over several decades through mainly agricultural lands before its final completion in 1815.

Centuries earlier the landscape would have been of vast wooded tracts; this was the Feckenham Forest which was the largest wood in the county. Villages like Hadzor and Hanbury started as forest clearings and the administration was in the hands of the Wardens of the Forest whose rules were very strict. One of the Wardens was Geoffrey Chaucer.

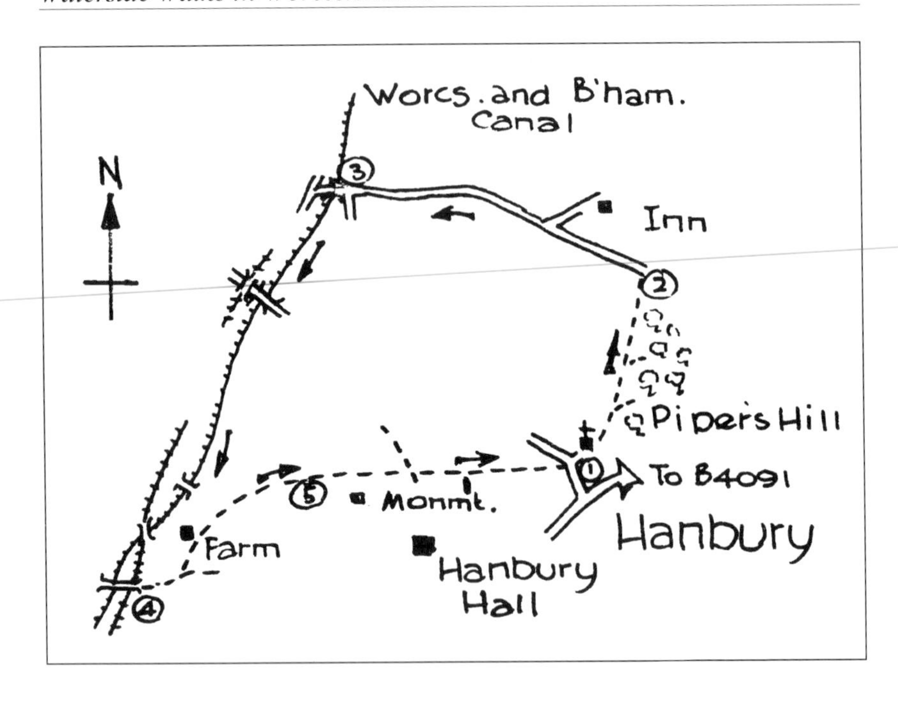

The forest was badly managed in medieval times when large areas of trees were felled to provide fuel for the Droitwich salt industry. Much of the land at this time was also sold illegally and used for agriculture which has resulted in the landscape we see today. However, many pockets of the old forest remain such as the oaks and beeches of Piper's Hill Wood which is on our route.

Early on the walk a fine hilltop church is passed. Although there is much work of the Norman masons incorporated in the building it has received more recent attention when it was used for radio recordings – here we are deep into the lands of *The Archers*. The church has some particularly attractive circular windows. There are also many memorials to the Vernon family who lived at Hanbury Hall and owned most of the lands around the village. The last Vernon to reside there (Sir George) has long gone and the building is now the property of the National Trust.

The pub (just off the route) is the Country Girl at Hanbury. This has been an inn since the middle of the 19th century. Although modernised the place retains much old world charm with oak beams and fires. Many unusual dishes will be found on the extensive menu alongside the old favourites such as ploughman's platter and home-made soups.

There is a wide range of beers available including Boddingtons and Marston's. The Country Girl has the normal opening hours. Telephone: 01527 821790.

- **HOW TO GET THERE:** The walk starts at Hanbury church. Turn off the B4091 a mile north of its junction with the B4090, 4 miles east of Droitwich. Continue along lanes to the church.
- **PARKING:** There is a car park by the church.
- **LENGTH OF THE WALK:** 4½ miles. Map: OS Landranger 150 Worcester and The Malverns (GR 953643).

THE WALK

1. Enter the churchyard and go along the path to the left of the church. Pass through a kissing gate and follow the arrowed path along a clear way to descend the hill. Pass through another kissing gate and continue along a path beside a wire fence.

Through a gate join a vehicle drive. Within 100 yards and just past a magnificent oak take a signed path bearing off left. There is now the lovely path through woodlands. Join another vehicle way by a cottage and keep ahead. Soon (by a reeded pool) leave the vehicle way to bear left. The path leads to a road.

2. Turn left. At a junction turn left (Astwood Lane). Note – the inn is to the right. After almost a mile a canal bridge is reached.

3. Walk down to the towing path and turn left to walk under the road. Go by several locks and under a road bridge then under bridges numbered 38 and 37. Immediately under the next bridge (No 36) climb the steps and stile.

4. Join a path that goes over the railway. Keep ahead along a bold tractor way. Within 300 yards and just after low electricity lines go left through a metal gate. Follow the left-hand hedge to pass through a corner gate by a farm.

Maintain the old heading with the house then a long low barn on the left. Keep ahead to go through a metal gate then proceed at the border of the field with woods away to the right. Continue along a stony tractor way through sheep pastures. Pass through a metal gate by game woods. Maintain the bearing past dew ponds to reach a junction of paths as National Trust grounds are entered.

Hanbury Hall

5. Two paths are signed over the stile ahead. Take the left-hand direction. Go by monuments (to faithful dogs!) and keep the direction over the parkland to a far stile by an ornate metal gate and (dried-up) pool.

Take the arrowed direction; we go by a small left-hand wood to a stile in the left-hand wire fence. Over this at once turn right so the wire fence is now on the right. Climb a corner stile and keep ahead with the church tower now acting as a beacon.

PLACES OF INTEREST NEARBY

Hanbury Hall (National Trust) is a fine William and Mary-style house dating from 1701. There are many features but perhaps the staircase designed by Sir James Thornhill is the gem. The 18th century formal gardens have recently been restored. The Hall is open from March to October with varying hours. Telephone: 01527 821214.

WALK 11

THE TEME AND A TALE OF THREE BRIDGES

The Teme rushes through its lovely wooded vale as though in a hurry to be swallowed up by the waters of the Severn. There have been at least three bridges carrying the highway across the river at Stanford Bridge, two of which we see today. The walk also nudges a lake with an interesting story.

Stanford Bridge

The original Stanford Bridge (nothing to do with Stamford Bridge – the home of Chelsea Football Club!) bore the inscription 'Praye for Humfrey Pakington Esquyer, borne in Stanford, which payed for the workmanshepe and making of this brygg the whiche was reared and made ye firste yere of ye rayne of Kyng Edward ye VI'. The spelling does not highlight the inadequacies of schooling in those distant days – it is the Tudor style!

That bridge, built by John Nash, was replaced in 1905 by a rather

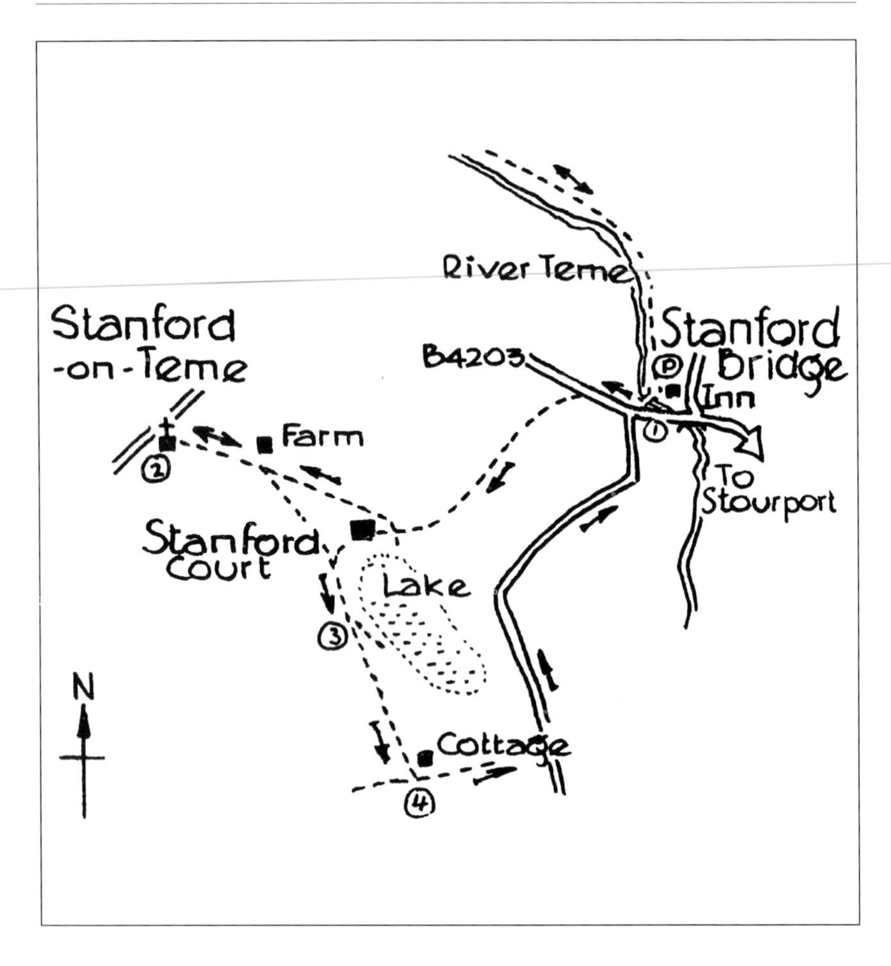

fine cast-iron arched structure. Fine it may be but its width was only suitable for the horse and cart and its usefulness was not long lasting. Now there is a modern utilitarian bridge but the old one remains for walkers to admire.

Half a mile away, approached by an avenue of tall trees, is Stanford Court which overlooks a large lake. For 200 years this was the seat of the Salweys then the Winningtons. We read too of the 15 year old bride who married Francis Winnington – poor Anne had ten children before she died aged 34.

It was a Winnington who in 1769 decided that the view from the house would be enhanced if there was a large lake here. The trouble was the village church was in the middle of the site. Undismayed, he submerged the church under the waters and built a new church on a nearby hilltop!

Stanford Court with its magnificent 15-bay stables was restored after a fire in 1886. The house remains but is now the headquarters of a large timber company.

The black and white inn by the river is the Bridge Inn. There are fine grassy areas (including a caravan site) and plenty of benches and tables. This is a traditional country inn with no pretensions except to offer good basic food and drink. The pub is open at lunchtime from noon each day and from 7 pm in the evenings. Telephone: 01886 812771.

- **HOW TO GET THERE:** Stanford Bridge can be reached along the A451 then the B4203 west of Stourport-on-Severn.
- **PARKING:** There is a car park at the Bridge Inn (charge made for non-patrons).
- **LENGTH OF THE WALK:** 2½ miles (may be extended). Map: OS Landranger 138 Kidderminster and Wyre Forest area (GR 715658).

This magnificent barn at Stanford is in need of some tender loving care!

The Walk

1. From the pub car park walk along the old pensioned-off bridge to the main road. Turn right. A Victorian mill (now a house) is passed. Within a few hundred yards take a signed footpath over a stile and along the drive of Stanford Court.

At the end of the avenue (by the 'Welcome to Forest' sign) climb a stile to an arable field on the right. Follow the left-hand border of the field (with the timber works and the house on the left side) around corners to a fence stile to pastureland. Aim towards a ruined farm building. Keep just to the left of this building. Pass through a metal gate then climb the hill to the hilltop church. This is a fine viewpoint looking across to 'Jones's Folly' (the tall 1884 clock tower), Woodbury Hill (900 ft) and the great lake of Stanford Court.

2. Retrace your steps down the hill to the gate near the ruined farm building. Do not go through the gate but turn right with a left-hand wire fence. Climb a corner stile and take the arrowed direction through the garden of Stanford Court to a tarmac vehicle way.

Turn right, passing stables, and go through a gate. Within 300 yards leave the vehicle way to climb a step stile right.

3. Regain the old heading in the field, never far from the left-hand border. Climb a stile to the right of a far corner and continue in the same direction to climb another stile, Keep ahead to go over a brook. Cross a sheep pasture to a gate to the right of a cottage.

4. Turn left and continue to a lane. Turn left and follow the lane around corners to the B4203. Cross to the old bridge to return to the car park.

If a longer walk is required there is a nice riverside path along the bank of the River Teme.

Places of Interest Nearby

Witley Court is about 3 miles east along the B4203. The opulent Court was built during the years 1655-1837. Long the home of the Dudleys, it was the scene of great society social gatherings and soirées before a disastrous fire in 1937. The church was spared and is a splendid example of the colourful art in the baroque style. Telephone: 01299 896636.

WALK 12

SALWARPE: A WALK FROM AN 'ISLAND'

The guidebook says that the village of Salwarpe is almost on an island! This is well nigh imperceptible but the church and the few houses and cottages are 'squeezed' between the little River Salwarpe and the Droitwich Canal which share the valley. This walk sets out along the canal and returns beside sections of the river.

The Droitwich Canal

Salwarpe means 'sallow, winding stream' or 'by a twisted willow' depending on which dictionary one consults but what is not disputed is that the river is very saline. Just when the Salwarpe valley was found to be so salty is not known but certainly the Romans knew of the existence of this valuable mineral – so necessary for the preservation of food in far off days. Many salt-grinding mills were set up along the river, and on this walk we pass one of them, now converted to a house.

The Droitwich Canal (opened in 1767) was built by Brindley to take

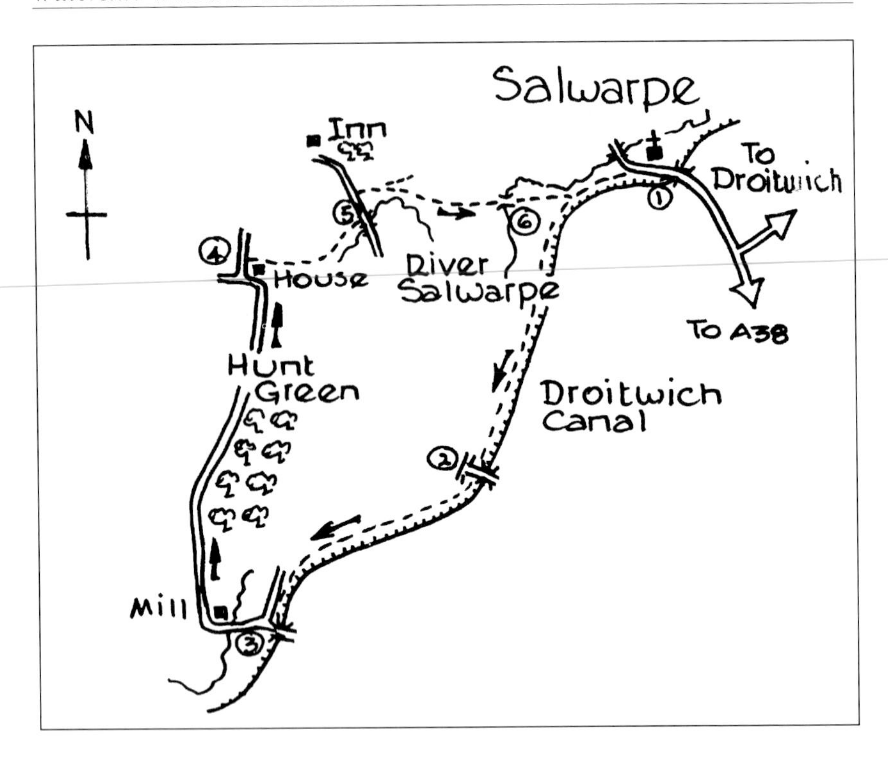

the salt to the Severn and to connect with the Worcester and Birmingham Canal for distribution in the Midlands. A score or so years ago the waterway became silted and un-navigable but the Droitwich Canal Trust (telephone: 0121 608 0296) is working to fully reopen it once more. Stretches have been cleared and boats can operate again to a limited degree. On the rest of the waterway nature rules, much to the pleasure of the reed warblers and long-tailed tits.

Before setting out on the walk glance over the bridge parapet to the canal running below in a deep cutting, then consider the amount of spoil which had to be removed when the waterway was built. There were no mechanical machines to help the work of the navvies and they depended entirely on shovels, picks and wheelbarrows.

The church by the start still has Norman stonework but, sadly, the arch was destroyed in one of those ardent Victorian restorations in 1848. Opposite the church are cottages which once housed the school, then the shop. Nearby is the 16th century Salwarpe Court which was the seat of the Talbots; we read that the Court was part of the marriage settlement of Catherine of Aragon to Prince Arthur.

There is no pub on the route but not far off (see point 4) is the Hadley Bowling Green Inn. The bowling green has given pleasure for 400 years and it is said that some of the Gunpowder Plot conspirators met at the inn. There is a lengthy menu and plenty of old favourites (and especially 'puds') to tempt a hungry walker. Banks's and Marston's ales are available as well as guest brews. Normal opening hours apply. Telephone: 01905 620294.

- **HOW TO GET THERE:** Turn westwards off the A38 by an inn at a crossroads, 300 yards south of the junction with the B4090 which runs from the centre of Droitwich. Follow the lane to Salwarpe.
- **PARKING:** There is a small car park near the church.
- **LENGTH OF THE WALK:** 3½ miles. Map: OS Landranger 150 Worcester and The Malverns (GR 874620).

THE WALK

1. Go along the lane with the church on the right. Within 100 yards turn left – the path is signed over a stile. Cross to climb another stile where two paths are signed. Turn left to go up steps to the canal. Turn right along the towing path.

2. By a lock and cottage cross the road to the indicated path opposite. Stay by the waterway and pass further locks. The canal is now badly reeded. Walk alongside the canal and a lane to reach a T-junction.

3. Turn right along Porter's Mill Lane. We soon come to the River Salwarpe and the mill. Go past the farmstead at Hunt Green.

4. Just beyond a road junction a path starts by Woodbury Cottage on the right. Note – keep ahead on the lane if you wish to visit the Hadley Bowling Green Inn. Afterwards you can turn left from the inn and rejoin the walk route at the bridleway in point 5.

On the path by Woodbury Cottage, walk over rough ground and beside garages then climb two stiles to an old orchard. Keep ahead to go over a rather hidden corner stile to a meadow and follow the arrowed direction. Go across a new footbridge to an arable field. Bear left to a wood. Keep the trees on the right; drop down to a gate onto a lane by the river.

5. Turn left then at once take a signed bridleway on the right. Walk

The reeds provide excellent cover for the wildlife on the canal

along a vehicle way. Within 200 yards leave the vehicle way to bear right along a fenced track. At the end climb a stile and bear left to climb the bank. Keep this heading up the ridge. Aiming to the right of the distant church tower walk over an often sown field to go over a footbridge across the river.

6. The direction of the path is now indicated to a stile to a plantation. Follow the clear path over stiles and through woods to rejoin the outward path. Retrace your steps to the car park.

PLACES OF INTEREST NEARBY

In the grounds of *Wichenford Court* (7 miles west of Salwarpe, approached along the A4133 and signed lanes) is a splendid 17th-century dovecote now maintained by the National Trust, which can be visited for a modest fee. It is open daily during the summer months. A mile along lanes eastwards from Wichenford is Monk Wood where there are marked nature trails and picnic places.

WALK 13

MARTLEY: A DAWDLE ALONG THE DARK RIVER

The River Teme always seems to be in a hurry to join the Severn. Our short walk is more sedate as there are tree-clothed hills to climb before descending to the pleasant waterside pathway.

Ham Bridge on the River Teme

The name of the River Teme is one of many from the same root. So we find the rivers Tame, Team and Thames and the Taff and Taf in Wales and even the Tegus. However one wonders why the root meaning 'dark river' is cognate with the Sanskrit 'Tamasa' – a tributary of the Ganges.

Where we walk along the Teme on this route the waters speed along eagerly towards the Severn and the sea. It has been a long journey – the river rises in the high hills near Newton in Wales then flows through Powys, Shropshire and Hereford before joining Britain's longest river near Worcester. The sinuous waterway we see twists a

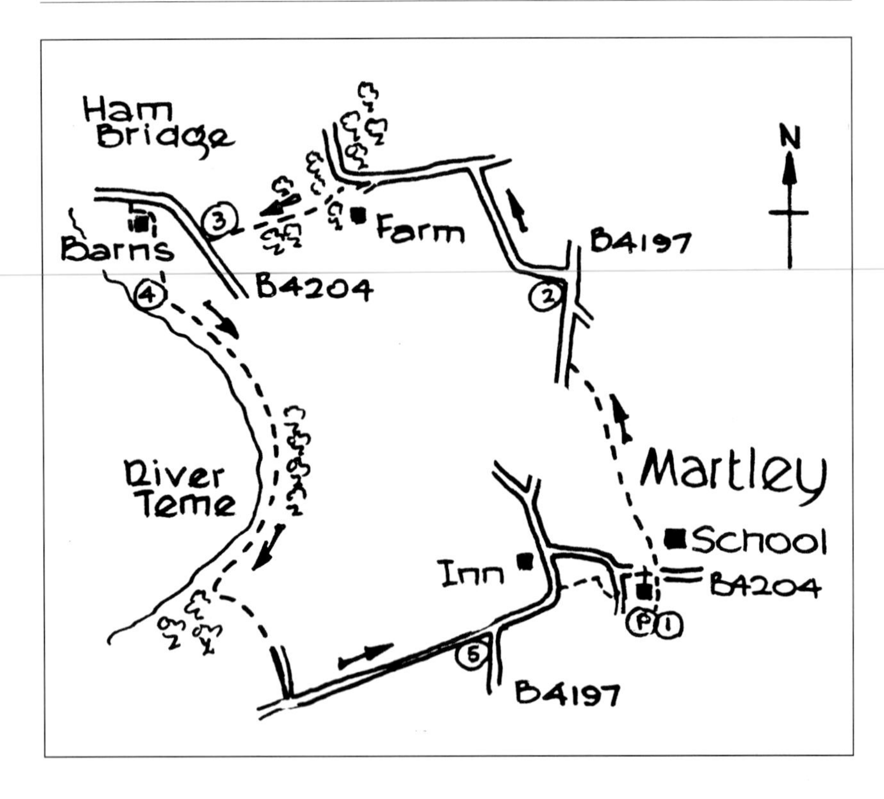

route through a valley often steep sided and clothed in orchards, the waterside meadows below, however, frequently becoming flooded in wintertime. It is not unusual to glimpse the buzzard – the largest of our common birds of prey – circling high above.

Martley (the wood of the martens) is our starting place. The tower of a fine 12th-century church overlooks the village. It was built of locally quarried red sandstone and fortunately escaped the attention of those sometimes rather over-enthusiastic Victorian restorers. Consequently a sympathetic restoration of 1909 found remarkable medieval wall paintings. One on the north nave wall depicts St Martin and the Beggar. The tower has a set of six bells which are the oldest complete peal in the land, dating from 1673.

The inn at Martley is the Crown and is a Banks's house. It has a large garden for enjoying those summer days and plenty of play equipment for youngsters. The two-course Sunday lunch is excellent value but there is always a very comprehensive menu and a 'specials' board. Normal pub opening hours apply. Telephone: 01886 888265.

- **HOW TO GET THERE:** Martley is at the junction of the B4197 and B4204, 6 miles north-west of Worcester.
- **PARKING:** There is a car park by the church.
- **LENGTH OF THE WALK:** 3 miles. Map: OS Landranger 150 Worcester and The Malverns (GR 756598).

The Walk

1. Walk from the car park through the churchyard. Keep ahead past the old school house to the main street at Martley. Cross to the signed path opposite and walk along a vehicle drive. At the end pass through a fence gap to at once enter a coppice.

Follow the clear path with school buildings to the right. At the end of the copse is a stile and a junction of paths. Our path is ahead across an open field, aiming towards a tall electricity pole and domed Rodge Hill. Go over a far stile then bear left over a sheep pasture to the main road. Turn right.

The road leading to Martley church

2. After 300 yards take a lane left. The narrow lane leads to a T-junction. Turn left along a way signed as a no through road. The lane borders a wood. Ignore the path signed to the right.

Just after the lane twists sharp right to almost double back on itself turn left down a rough vehicle track. Within a step or two our path is signed over a stile. In woods take the arrowed direction; descend through the trees then continue along the path which borders a meadow to a road.

3. Turn right for about 200 yards then turn left down a rough farm vehicle way which is signed as a footpath. (A little further along the road is Ham Bridge. Built in 1842 this replaced a rather dangerous ford crossing of the Teme a mile downstream at Kingswood.) Within a few steps along the vehicle way turn left then right to go around barns. Follow the waymarked route over the field to the river.

4. Turn left along the bankside path. The path soon is above the river and goes through woods (once orchards) then joins a lane. Keep the direction to a T-junction. Turn left to the B4197.

5. Turn left for 300 yards. As the road bends left take a signed path on the right. Follow the waymarked path through a paddock then right across a field to a lane by the car park.

Places of Interest Nearby

In *Upper Broadheath*, 5 miles from Martley to the south-east, is the birthplace of arguably England's greatest composer Sir Edward Elgar. The humble cottage which houses a fascinating museum is open daily and is well signposted. Telephone: 01905 333224.

WALK 14

SHERNAL GREEN AND ODDINGLEY: A CANALSIDE ODYSSEY

From Shernal Green, a stroll across pastureland takes us to the peaceful village of Oddingley. The route then joins the towpath where, at the Dunhampstead tunnel, we follow in the footsteps of the bargees and divert over the hill before dropping down to the canal once more.

The churchyard at Oddingley

The fortunes of the Worcester and Birmingham canal suffered when the railway came towards the end of the 19th century. There was once a thriving goods yard at Dunhampstead where the waterway nudged the main rail route – and the canal had the problem of the high hill which necessitated a 230 yard long tunnel. To negotiate this the towing donkeys and horses had to be unhitched and walked, like us, over the upland. The bargees would then have the hard work of 'legging' the craft through – they would lie on their backs and 'walk' along the sides of the tunnel. One can see the benefits of a speedy railway!

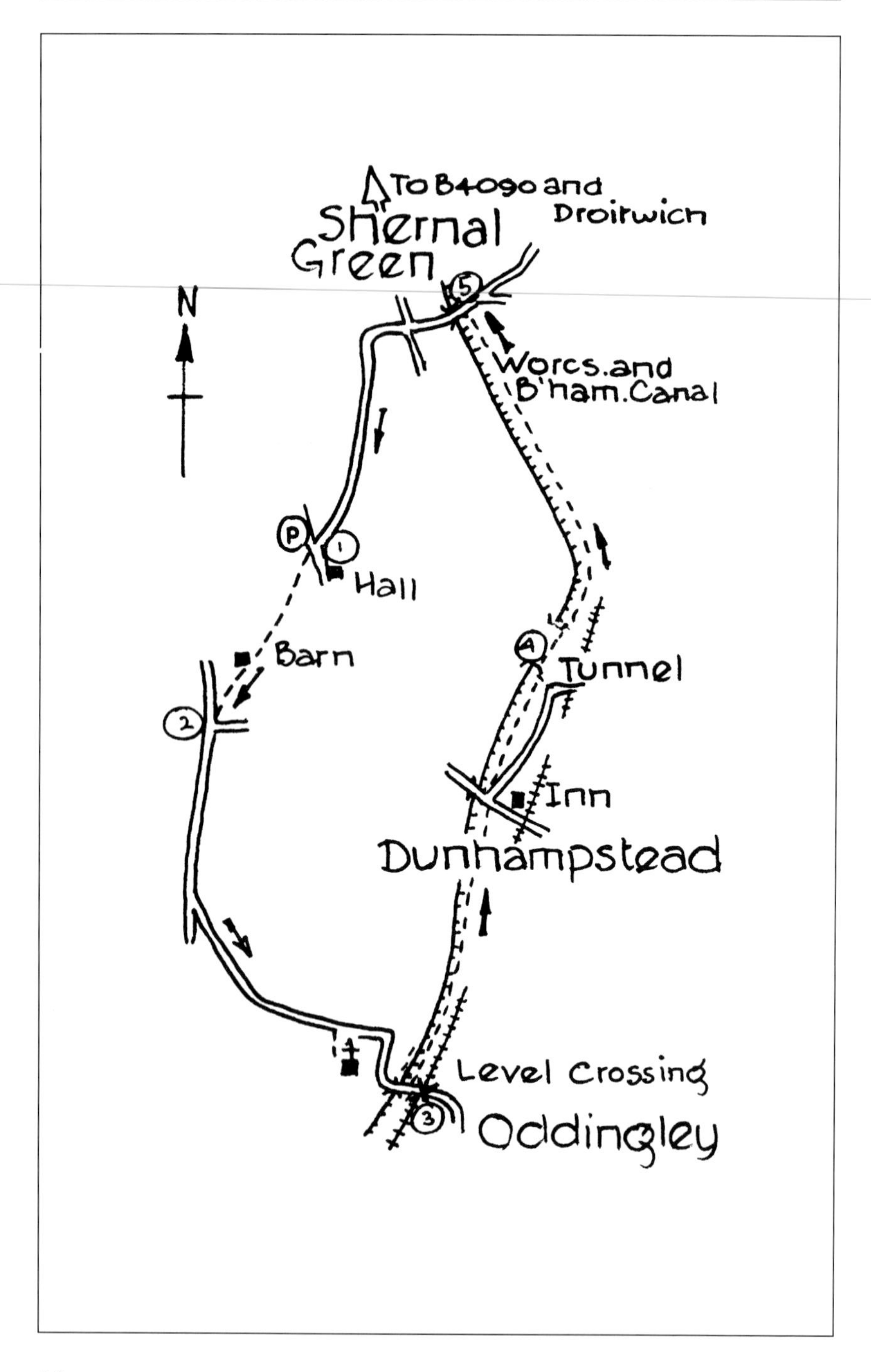
To B4090 and
Droitwich
Shernal
Green
N
Worcs. and
B'ham. Canal
Hall
Barn
Tunnel
Inn
Dunhampstead
Level Crossing
Oddingley

The area where we walk was on the drovers' route from Wales to London and the south. The verges alongside the lanes are very large as they provided grazing for the cattle on their journey. Inns were established for the men and they are often distinguished as drovers' hostelries by the fir trees planted outside (hence the name of the inn on the route of our walk).

The village of Oddingley is visited; this was an old Saxon settlement (the 'place of Odda's people'). It is a scattered community and may have originally been a collection of squatters' cottages. It has a tranquil 'away from it all' feeling. But how different it all was on Midsummer's Day in 1806 when the vicar (the Rev George Parker) was murdered.

The lovely church, largely rebuilt in 1851, has a 17th century tower. It overlooks the fields towards the canal and railway and contains a font that is 400 years old.

The Firs Inn at Dunhampstead is a fine country inn with a great reputation for good food – necessary really as it is rather isolated and well off main highways. There are always 'specials of the day' and the traditional fare is excellent for hungry walkers. Banks's beer is always available, alongside other brews. Normal opening hours apply during the week but the pub is open all day at weekends. Telephone: 01905 774094.

- **HOW TO GET THERE:** From the B4090 just east of Droitwich take the lane through Hadzor to Shernal Green, turning right to the village hall.
- **PARKING:** By or in the village hall car park or along the nearby cul de sac lane.
- **LENGTH OF THE WALK:** 3½ miles. Map: OS Landranger 150 Worcester and The Malverns (GR 913607).

THE WALK

1. At the road junction at the start of the walk there is a stile to climb. Take the indicated direction of the footpath to walk at the right-hand border of a pasture, passing just to the right of a water pump. In the next field again walk at the right-hand border. Keep on this direction to climb a stile by a barn. Keep ahead (still right-hand borders) to a stile onto a lane by a junction.

2. Turn left to keep the old heading. Within ½ mile bear left along a lane, signed to Netherwood. Soon take a way to the right along the

Full steam ahead near Oddingley

drive to visit Oddingley church then retrace your steps to the lane and turn right. Go over the level crossing – this is a main line and the gates are still opened manually!

3. After a few steps the canal bridge is reached. Gain the towing path and walk northwards with the water on the left side. Go under bridges (for the inn at Dunhampstead leave the canal at the first road bridge). A hundred yards before the canal tunnel the path goes up the embankment. Climb to a wide track and a junction of ways. Maintain the old heading to the entrance to Tunnel Farm.

4. Bear left along a wide vehicle track. Within a hundred yards go right off the vehicle way to drop down again to the canal and resume walking along the towing path.

5. Go under the bridge at Shernal Green and climb to the road. Turn right to go over the water. Continue directly over at a crossroads and follow the lane to the start.

Places of Interest Nearby

Droitwich is a fascinating town. Its fame and fortune were founded on salt, so necessary for the preservation of food for hundreds of years. The water in the brine baths was said to be 40 per cent more salty than the Red Sea. Some of the older buildings are leaning due to the extraction of underground salt. A noted building is Chateau Impney. Now an hotel it was built in a French style by the 'Salt King' John Corbett to please his Parisian wife.

WALK 15

KNIGHTWICK: NUDGING THE TEME

This walk goes along the valley of the River Teme – we are only by the river for a short distance but the route continues as a splendid jaunt over a high ridge. The views therefore are over two vales – the Severn and the Teme.

The village of Knightwick

The road up the ridge is said to be one of the steepest in the country and it is a puffing climb for the rambler. The hill is clothed in deciduous woods which are an especial delight in autumntime. The long distance path of the Worcestershire Way which wends a course through the county also goes over the hill. We use the route for a while – it is well waymarked with a Worcestershire pear symbol.

The walk starts at the little hamlet of Knightwick. Here the old bridge called Knightsford is now only for walkers after having been found unsafe for motor vehicles. The new bridge is downstream a few yards so restoring peace to the little community.

The ancient crossing place was by means of a ford near the old bridge. Here a prehistoric track ran – it was to become a drovers' road along which cattle were led from Wales to the southern markets. In later years it was a main stagecoach route between the capital and Aberystwyth.

When the Teme ford was impassable travellers would be accommodated in inns each side. The Flying Horse was on the west bank and the Talbot on the other bank. In 1886 the river was exceptionally high and the flood water engulfed the little community; the height of the water can be seen on a stone by the church. The place of worship is from the 19th century but has some work of the Normans including their font.

The Talbot of the two travellers' inns still remains; although the building dates from the 14th century it is now a fine modernised hostelry where the landlord takes a pride in his summer show of flowers. The inn is advertised as being 'beside one of the prettiest and least known of English rivers'. The 'full walker's breakfast', available all day, will set you up well to climb that high Ankerdine Hill! The Talbot is open 11 am to 11 pm daily (Sunday from 12 noon). Telephone: 01886 821235.

- **HOW TO GET THERE:** Knightwick is 7 miles west of Worcester, at the junction of the A44 and B4197.
- **PARKING:** On the old road in front of the Talbot.
- **LENGTH OF THE WALK:** 4 miles. Map: OS Landranger 150 Worcester and The Malverns (GR 733560).

THE WALK

1. Beside the inn take a signed path which goes along a farm vehicle way. Go past tree plantations and orchards then the track runs alongside the river. Follow the way past a farm. The track is now a quiet lane with the 600 ft Berrow Hill which is crowned with the ramparts of an Iron Age hillfort on the left.

2. Turn left when the lane reaches the B4197. Go past one road junction. Just before the next take a path (waymarked with the 'pear' Worcestershire Way sign) on the right.

3. Follow the edge of the right-hand border of the field. At a waymark post go right over a stile then at once left so now walking beside a left-hand hedge. Go over a corner stile then turn left to climb another.

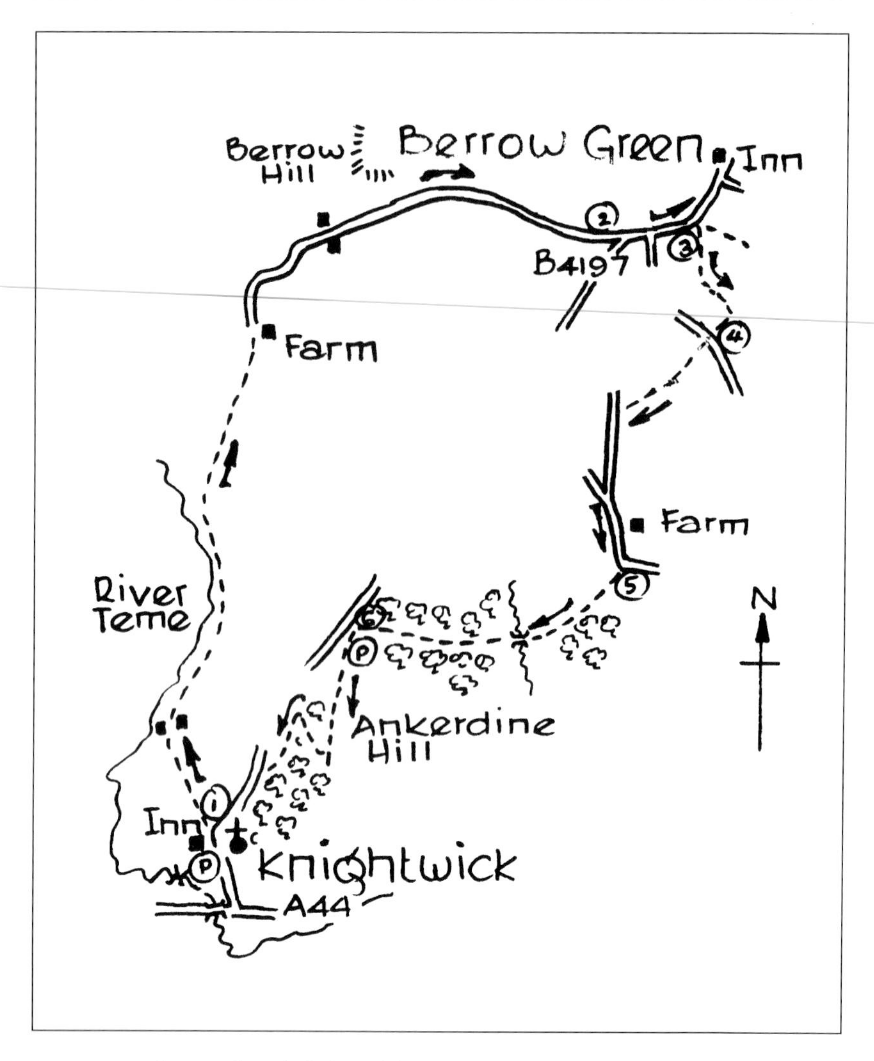

Continue alongside a left-hand hedge.

Just before a corner turn 90° right and climb the rise (ignoring a path signed by a gate on the left). Climb a stile to a lane.

4. Go straight over and follow the arrowed way over a field that is sometimes arable. At a lane turn left and keep ahead at a junction and pass farms.

5. As the lane bears left go through gates right. Gradually leave the left-hand border of the field. Go over a brook to woods and follow the clear path through the trees. At a junction of paths go right and follow the main path uphill to a stile to a hill pasture. Keep climbing to go through a kissing gate next to a cottage.

6. At once turn left. The vehicle way leads to a picnic site; keep ahead through a white metal gate. Beyond a cottage the vehicle way becomes a footpath through woodlands. Carefully look for a waymark post directing us down steps to the right. The path borders a wooden fence. At a Y-junction take the left hand fork to a road. Turn left to Knightwick.

Places of Interest Nearby

Two miles along lanes to the south (signs to Alfrick) there is a *Nature Reserve*. Information boards indicate what to look for. Benches and tables are provided for picnics and there is a car park. Alfrick was once a hop growing area but most of the cowled oast houses where the hops were dried have now been converted to private houses.

WALK 16

A WORCESTERSHIRE PIDDLE

The name of this little brook always raises a smile; the word actually comes from the German meaning 'low land or a fen or marsh'. Certainly the stream meanders in a valley – and you can ponder on the aptness of the name as you walk beside the Piddle on your way from Flyford Flavell towards the peaceful village of Grafton Flyford.

The path through the fields near Grafton Flyford

The waters of the Piddle Brook rise on the ridge on the eastern borders of Worcestershire and flow into the Avon and thence the Severn. There is another 'Piddle' in Dorset and like our brook this has given its name to several villages and hamlets, such as Piddletrenthide. Perhaps the most famous place is Tolpuddle where the 'Martyrs' lived and rebelled.

Our walk starts at Flyford Flavell; Flavell was the name of the Norman lord and Flyford was the track through the Feckenham Forest. Now the area is mainly agricultural; many of the trees were cut down to supply the insatiable need of the Droitwich salt industry. Sizeable woods remain and we walk past Grafton Wood.

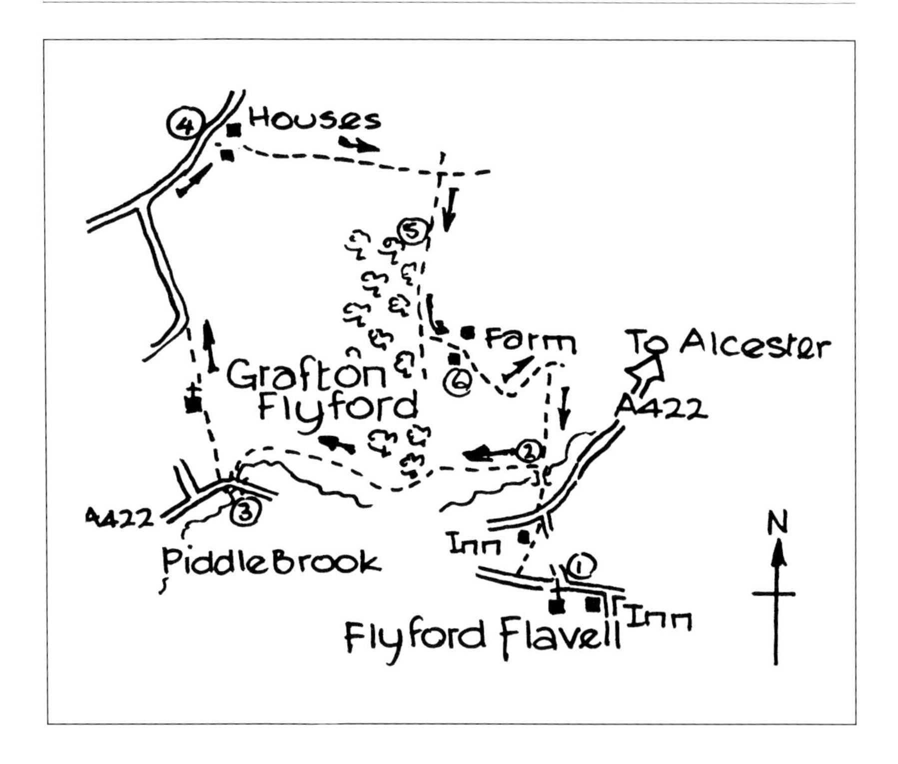

Grafton Flyford is a very remote village although guidebooks written several decades ago gave bold mention of a new town planned around the little hilltop church. Obviously the grand plan never materialised so we are left with a lovely quiet countryside. The church is from the 13th century although much rebuilding took place in 1875. The medieval window glass survived. Nearby is a fine black and white timbered house so typical of the county.

The Boot Inn at Flyford Flavell is a well-kept pub with a menu of traditional and more unusual dishes. The steak and kidney pies are especially good. Normal opening hours apply. Telephone: 01386 462658.

- **HOW TO GET THERE:** Halfway along the A422 between Alcester and Worcester take the lane southwards to Flyford Flavell.
- **PARKING:** On quiet roadsides in the village.
- **LENGTH OF THE WALK:** 4 miles. Map: OS Landranger 150 Worcester and The Malverns (GR 980549).

The Walk

1. Walk westwards from the centre of Flyford Flavell, passing the school shop and church. Keep ahead at a junction. Within 300 yards take a signed footpath on the right. In the pasture follow the indicated direction to a stile by a road junction.

Cross the main road to climb the opposite stile. Again take the arrowed direction to cross the field to a bridge over Piddle Brook.

2. Across the water turn left with the brook on your left side. Climb a stile; here is a junction of paths. Keep ahead to stay by the brook.

The brook is then away to the left for a while as the path goes to a wood (Grafton Wood). Climb a stile and turn left then right at a fence. Within a few yards go over a stile; immediately turn right so the fence is now on your right side. Just after a fence stile (which you do not climb) towards the end of the wood go through a gateway (no gate). Keep the old direction alongside a scrubby wood to the far end of a pasture.

Go over a wire fence – now we are back near the Piddle. Go past a barn (on the left) and a stile (do not climb) to stay by a left-hand hedge. Follow the border of the field and brook to a plank bridge. Maintain the heading through further fields and follow the waymarked route to a stile onto the main road.

3. Turn right for a few steps then take another path over a stile right. Aim for a church tower, never far from the right-hand hedge. Climb a stile to a car park by the old school and continue ahead through a little gate to the churchyard.

Walk to the right of the church to an old metal kissing gate to a house drive (notice the splendid black and white house nearby). Cross to the stile and maintain the direction over another. Gradually bear right as the path drops downhill to a very far corner by ponds. Keep ahead a few steps to go through a green metal gate to a lane. Turn right. Go past a junction and stay on the lane for a further ½ mile.

4. By a house called Woodend take a signed bridleway on the right. Go along the house drive then keep ahead along a fenced way (hedge on the left). Go through a metal gate and maintain the heading.

Pass through a far bridle gate and keep ahead. After passing through a corner yellow gate turn half right in a vast sheep pasture. Walk just to the left of an isolated oak.

The friendly guardians of the bridge over Piddle Brook

5. Climb a stile at the corner of a wood. In a meadow follow the arrowed direction, now walking along the Wychavon Way. Climb two stiles close together in a copse to re-enter pastureland. Again follow the right-hand border of a wood. In a corner enter the woods then return to a meadow again with trees to the right. Ignore other paths and keep ahead. In a distant corner follow the edge of the field left, now walking towards barns.

6. Climb a stile right. Bear left then right to join a house drive. Follow this over a cattle grid. The drive then bears left. Just before another cattle grid climb a stile right. Follow the left-hand hedge downhill to climb a stile by the Piddle Brook. Retrace your steps to Flyford Flavell.

Places of Interest Nearby

Spetchley Park, 6 miles west along the A422, has been the home of the Berkeleys for over three centuries. The present house (built in the early years of the 19th century and not open to the public) is surrounded by a deer park and a fine garden. Telephone: 01905 3452313.

WALK 17

CLEEVE PRIOR: A STROLL ALONG THE AVON

There are many interesting features on this ramble; the river is a favourite with holiday captains and crews and there is always much activity to watch, but perhaps the highlight is the massive tithe barn in Middle Littleton. It was built on the orders of Abbot Ombersley of Evesham in 1376 and is now in the care of the National Trust.

Cruising down the Avon

Cleeve Prior where we start was built on a high ridge 200 ft above the flood plain of the Avon. The market garden industry of old (the common having been enclosed in 1775) has somewhat declined but no doubt the river was once used to convey the produce to the markets. There was a mill (at the end of Mill Lane of course) and a wharf but now after its demolition following the Second World War not a stone remains to tell the tale.

In the river by the mill (where old guidebooks tell us there was a

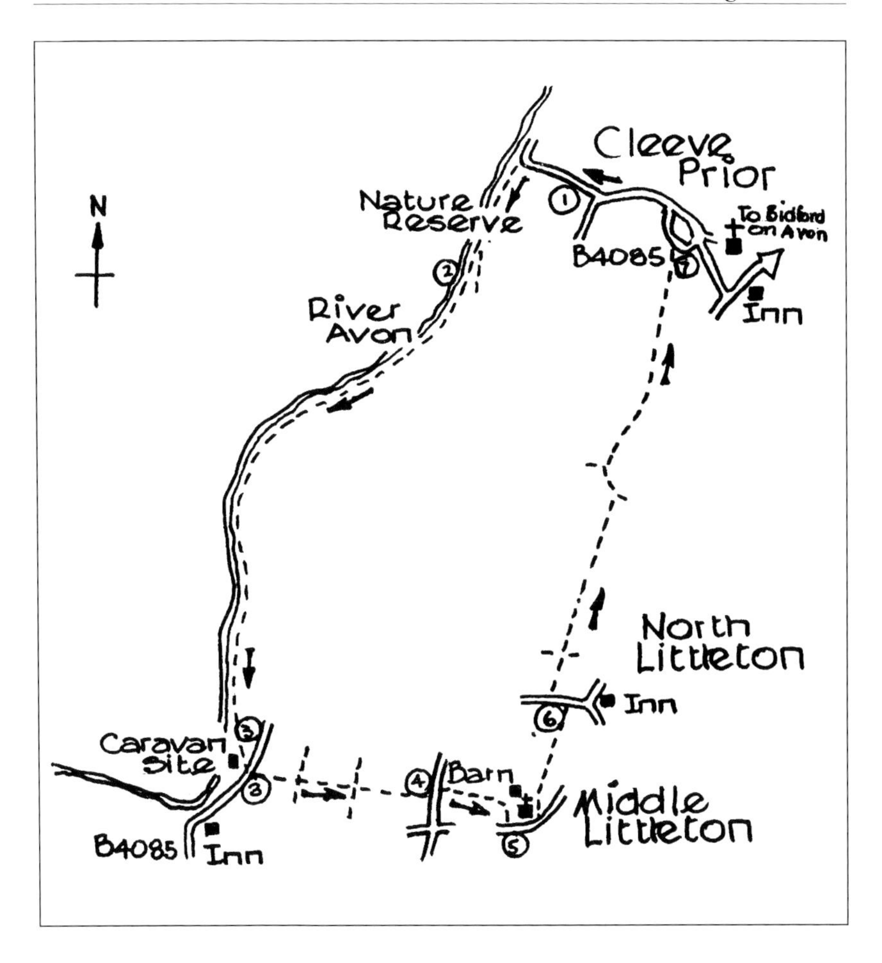

footbridge spanning to the opposite bank) it is thought that many of Simon de Montfort's troops perished trying to cross the speeding waters after the Battle of Evesham (see Walk 18).

What we can see is the Manor House; in this building Thomas Bushell found a hiding place when he was sought for providing Charles I with money when the Royal Mint was in the hands of the Parliamentarians. He died in 1674 and was buried in Westminster Abbey for his 'Services to the Nation'.

The village has a splendid church with much Norman work; St Andrew's has a 15th century tower which was of strategic importance as a look out tower and the evidence is there that the hard local grey stone at the base was used by the archers for sharpening arrows.

The King's Arms has been the village inn for many years; a beam inside is dated 1542 so it is certain that Thomas Bushell would have known the warm welcome that we still receive today. The walls are still perforated – holes for the dovecote; 100 years ago there were said to be 'hundreds of pigeon holes'. A good selection of beers is available including Whitbread and Boddingtons. The place boasts selling 'the best chips in the county' but for the more health-conscious a wide choice of salads is offered. There is a garden for those summer days and the year round opening hours are 11.30 am to 2.30 pm and 6.30 pm to 11 pm. Telephone: 01789 773335.

- **HOW TO GET THERE:** Cleeve Prior is 2 miles south of Bidford-on-Avon on the B4085.
- **PARKING:** Quiet roadside is available.
- **LENGTH OF THE WALK:** 4½ miles. Map: OS Landranger 150 Worcester and The Malverns (GR 083496).

THE WALK

1. Walk along the cul de sac lane of Mill Lane. At the crown of a hill turn left along a signed bridleway and into the nature reserve. There are now fine views over the Avon valley. Within ½ mile there is a division of ways (take care as the waymark post may be missing). Bear right along a clear descending footpath with open views over a lake right.

2. On meeting the river climb a stile. The path now borders the river, soon with a large fishing pool on the left. A series of stiles shows our way – staying near the river. A 'weir' notice is reached. Go over a stile and plank bridge. Walk through scrubland to a vehicle drive which you follow through a caravan site to a road.

3. Turn left then at once right. The unsigned path is through an old gateway (no gate). In the often arable field turn half left, aiming towards a stile just seen in the opposite boundary below the ridge. Over the stile take the arrowed direction to climb the steep ridge. On the top go over another stile and cross a track to the green path opposite. Walk through fields – some of sweet smelling herbs in season. Go over a stile and continue to a road.

4. Take the signed path opposite and keep by a right-hand hedge. Maintain the heading over a stile to climb a far corner stile by a stone cottage. Follow the vehicle way (with the entrance to the tithe barn to the left) to a road at Middle Littleton.

5. Turn left to pass the entrance gate to the church. A few steps further pass through a metal kissing gate to the churchyard. Walk to the right of the church and through a metal gate. Keep ahead to climb a stile to a meadow. Maintain the heading to go over a stile just to the left of a black barn. Follow the arrowed path to walk beside houses to Arrow Lane.

6. Turn left (there is an inn to the right). Within 300 yards take a signed path over a stile right. Keep ahead over stiles and then along a vehicle way for 40 yards. When the vehicle way swings left through a gate keep the old direction to a stile by trees.

The impressive tithe barn at Middle Littleton

Over the stile turn right then at once left to keep at the edge of an arable field. Pick up another tractor way and follow it. We pass the magnificent project of a new tree-fringed village green to mark the Millennium. By houses go right then take a signed path left after a step or two to an estate road to the main street at Cleeve Prior.

7. Turn left to Mill Lane (or right to the inn).

Places of Interest Nearby

Ragley Hall is about 4 miles north of Cleeve Prior. The Hall is the home of the Earl of Hertford and there is a magnificent park with an especially noted heronry. The Hall and park are open to visitors during the summer months from Easter and children love the extended adventure playground. Telephone: 01789 762090. *Coughton Court* (7 miles north of Cleeve Prior) is in the care of the National Trust. It is a magnificent house from the Tudor period, long the home of the Throckmorton family and closely associated with the Gunpowder Plot. There is a fine central gateway. The estate borders the River Arrow where there are riverside walks and a picnic place. The opening hours are rather complex – best to check. Telephone: 01789 400777.

WALK 18

EVESHAM: THE AVON NOOSE

The stretch of the Avon on this walk played an important part in the history of the kingdom. The actual site of the Battle of Evesham (1265) is on private land but we can gaze up at the isolated hill and realise the hazards of the river for escaping troops.

The River Avon at Evesham

In 1265 Simon de Montfort – the 'father of English liberty' – fought out his last fight of the Barons' War. He was encamped to the north of a sharp loop in the River Avon. When an army was seen on a hill overlooking Evesham Simon thought that it was his son (also Simon), victorious after defeating the King's army at Kenilworth. But it was Prince Edward's forces who were at the gates of the town. Too late Simon realised the enemy were at hand but there was no escape with the waters of the Avon (swollen by a storm) almost surrounding him. The battle lasted only three hours; many of Simon's troops plunged into the river and subsequently perished. Unfortunately, the actual site of the great fight is on private property and cannot be visited. However,

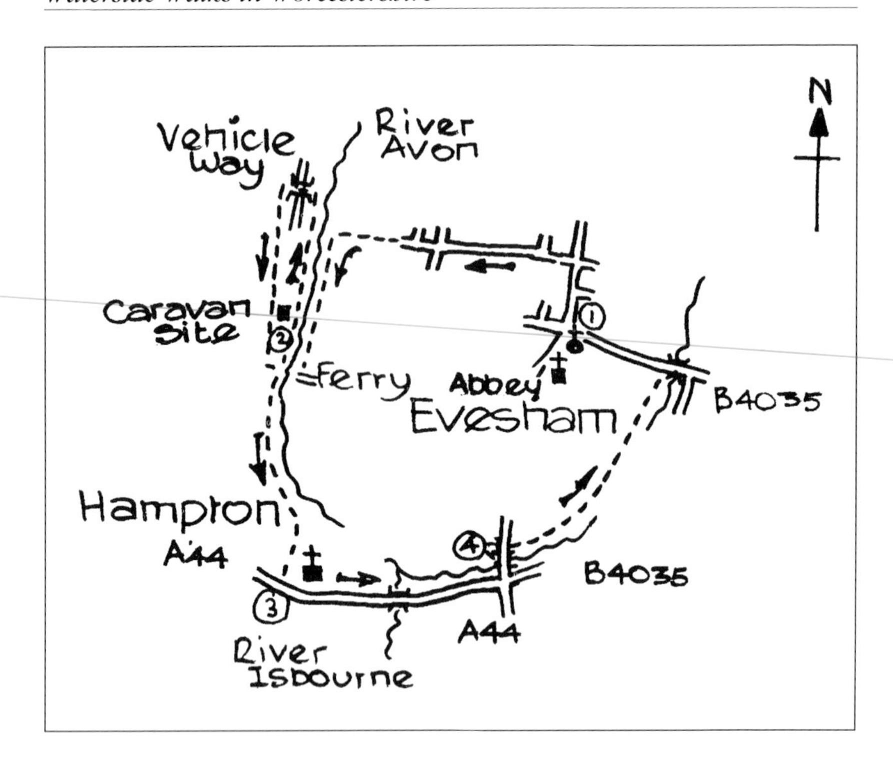

the route of the walk is along the banks of the Avon and we can gaze up to the heights above and visualise the battle. Many of Simon's forces tried to find sanctuary in the Abbey but despite the protestations of the monks they were killed.

The importance of Simon de Montfort is revealed in a plinth on the site of the Abbey. It reads 'Here were buried the remains of Simon De Montfort pioneer of representative government'. It was erected to commemorate the 700th anniversary of his death.

The Abbey was founded in AD 714; the Bell Tower which proudly overlooks Evesham was only completed in 1539 – the year the Abbey was dissolved on the orders of Henry VIII. Many comment how unsuspecting Abbot Lichfield must have been to have built the opulent tower when storm clouds were gathering.

There were once many ferry crossings of the Avon but with the availability of motor transport only a few remain. Hampton Ferry is popular with those living in Hampton who have to travel to Evesham to work. But note that the ferry does not operate in the months of January and February.

There is an abundance of inns, restaurants and cafés in Evesham to suit all tastes (and pockets). The Ducks Don't Float in the central Market Place at Evesham is a popular pub. The unusual name is matched by its decor – a wide range of posters decorate the walls. The food includes the offer of two meals for a fiver and beers available include Worthington and Boddingtons. The opening hours are 11.30 am to 11 pm daily except Sunday (12 noon to 10.30 pm). Telephone: 01386 494661.

- **HOW TO GET THERE:** Evesham is on the A46 south of Alcester. Approaching from the north, take the A4184 into the centre of the town.
- **PARKING:** There are several public car parks (fee paying).
- **LENGTH OF THE WALK:** 3½ miles. Map: OS Landranger 150 Worcester and The Malverns (GR 037437).

Fladbury Mill, downstream of Evesham

The Walk

Note: As previously mentioned, the ferry does not operate in January or February, so this walk must be left for the months of March to December.

1. Walk north along the broad High Street. Turn left down Avon Street which leads to the river. Turn left to the ferry. Across the water turn right.

2. Follow the edge of the Avon with a caravan park on the left then through the rather untidy area beyond. We leave the river to walk alongside a marshy area (on the right side). Just before a stile into woods turn left to walk uphill through bushes to a bridge over a vehicle way. Turn left to walk never far from the hidden vehicle way (on your left side) to return to the ferry. Do not cross the river.

Follow the path ahead to stay by the Avon. Climb a stile and maintain the direction over another. Follow a vehicle way to the main road.

3. Turn left past Hampton church then cross the little River Isbourne. What is strange about this river (which once powered many mills) is that it is one of the few rivers in the kingdom which flows north.

4. At a busy road junction turn left a few steps then take the path which goes under the main road. Follow the riverside path to return to the town.

Places of Interest Nearby

There are so many places to visit in *Evesham* or you could call in at one, or more, of the many wayside market gardens outside the town – the *Vale of Evesham* is the garden of the Midlands. Especially beautiful are the orchards in spring when there are signposted 'blossom trails'.

WALK 19

CROOME PARK: THE LAKES OF 'CAPABILITY' BROWN

In the grounds of Croome Court at Croome d'Abitot which was the seat of the Earls of Coventry is an inscription on an urn reading: 'To the memory of Launcelot Brown who by the powers of his inimitable and creative genius, formed this garden scene out of a morass'. We can enjoy the serpentine lake created by the 'genius' on this walk.

The lake in Croome Park

It is said that 'Capability' Brown had much to do with the plans of the great house (built 1750-1) and the church which we visit on the route. The cost was enormous – in the region of £400,000. It was at Croome that Brown made his reputation as it was his first commission to design a complete landscape; it was to become a model for the next half century.

Robert Adam was called upon to mould the interior of the house.

Sadly, much of Adam's work has been dismantled over the years (the place has been used as a school and by a religious organisation) and much of the old beauty neglected.

A significant area of the park was acquired by the National Trust in 1996 thanks to a large grant from Lottery funds and now there is a ten-year restoration plan under way. Part of the old western pleasure grounds including the lakeside garden are open daily (except Monday, Tuesday and Wednesday) to the public during the summer months from May until September.

We can see the house exterior in its garden setting. The church is owned by the Churches Conservation Trust and is open at weekends, also during the summer months. It was sited as an eye-catcher on a little hill by the 2nd Earl of Coventry and contains splendid work by Adam and Grinling Gibbons.

We are abruptly made aware of more modern times as Croome Park overlooks the old RAF airfield of Defford. This is now a vast early-warning complex with an array of huge radar dishes and 'golf balls'.

There is no pub on the actual route but there is a good path from the park to the village of Kinnersley where you can visit the Royal Oak. They still talk in the cosy bar about the time when a Grand National winner was trained here. The beer is from Bass; the food is well worth the detour for a hungry rambler especially the jacket potatoes brimming with assorted fillings. The speciality when I called was the delicious sausage and mash with red wine gravy. Opening hours are 12 noon to 10.30 pm daily. Telephone: 01905 371482.

- **HOW TO GET THERE:** A mile or so north of Upton-upon-Severn turn eastwards off the A38 to the hamlet of High Green.
- **PARKING:** Quiet roadside parking is available by the road junction in the centre of the hamlet by the sign for Westfield Farm.
- **LENGTH OF THE WALK:** 3½ miles. Map: OS Landranger 150 Worcester and The Malverns (GR 875451).

The Walk

1. By the road junction there is a stile with two paths signed. Take the right-hand path across the field. Go over a far stile and footbridge to a farm vehicle way. Nearby are two delightful carved pillars. (The park has many folly gothic ruins, obelisks and temples – further work of 'Capability' Brown to enhance the scene.)

2. Cross to the signed footpath which goes right along a vehicle way. We pass near a lake which is surrounded by bluebells in the spring. We soon have our first view across the fields to the left of Croome Court with its four corner towers.

3. The vehicle way goes sharp left then right. Nearing buildings we go through a kissing gate left and take the arrowed direction. (Note – for the pub at Kinnersley go through the gate right just before the buildings.)

We soon have the elongated mile-long lake on our left. The path goes over the open field to reach a delightful spot at the end of the lake. Follow the clear path over the bridge and by a waterfall then around the end of the lake. Do not climb the stile right.

Pick up a path at the end of the wood with a wire fence on the left.

The elegant gateway leading to Croome Court

We come to another Greek-style folly and pass to the left of this along National Trust signed paths. At a junction of paths (a National Trust sign is near) veer left to a field. Bear right to pick up a wire fence and a wood on the right.

4. At a corner of the wood maintain the old heading over the open field. The radar station is in the vale to the right. Pick up a line of oak trees then the path borders a right-hand wood. Maintain the heading to a road. Turn left to pass a fine arch across the road that leads to the great house. Continue for about 400 yards.

5. Take a signed path on the left which leads directly to a churchyard and Croome church. Turn right past a fine wooden seat. Through a gateway turn left. Follow the edge of the field to pick up a tractor way at the side of a left-hand wood.

As the tractor way turns sharp right keep ahead through a corner hedge gap. Go over a plank bridge and stay by a left-hand wood.

6. At the end of the wood go through a hedge gap to a field path. Head towards the chimneys of a distant house. The path leads to High Green.

Places of Interest Nearby

The interesting Georgian town of *Pershore* is 4 miles to the east along lanes. There is a fine 14th century packhorse bridge but the gem of the town is the *Abbey*. Although much of the original building has been destroyed by time or neglect what remains has lovely work of the Norman builders and the tower is a landmark for miles. About 8 miles north is *Worcester* with its celebrated cathedral. It was said to have been King John's favourite city and he was buried in the cathedral. Worcester china and porcelain are world-known and the city also is a pleasant place to shop. For cricketers the New Road ground is in a picturesque setting by the river.

WALK 20

STROLLING BY THE SILVER SEVERN

This walk is alongside Britain's longest river. The Severn rises on the Plynlimon mountain in North Wales. By the time it reaches Upton it is wide and often cannot cope with all the water coming from the uplands and the tributaries. Flooding near Upton-upon-Severn results in verdant meadows brimming with wild flowers through which we stroll at the end of the route.

The River Severn at Upton

In far off medieval times most of the nation's merchandise was conveyed by rivers. Canals had not been built and packhorse traffic was limited. From these times until the arrival of the Canal Age towards the end of the 18th century the river trade was paramount and the River Severn was to carry more traffic than any other river in the land.

Near the sea was Bristol – then the second port in England – but further upstream were inland ports such as Upton and Bewdley from whence the goods were conveyed by land. Items were taken from the ocean-going vessels along the shallower waters in special flat-bottomed boats. Although some had sails most of the power came from the bow-hauliers – teams of men who pulled the heavy craft by ropes.

Upton-upon-Severn is a fascinating town. It is dominated by a 'salt-cellar' 14th century tower; this is all that remains of the old church that was destroyed in a Civil War skirmish. The bridge was damaged but enemy troops utilised planks to span the gap and surprise the Royalists who were encamped in the building. This old bridge (which was in line with the main street of the town) was replaced in 1853. It was here that the Bridge Parliament met – a gathering of all who used the waterway. This bridge survived for about 100 years. Now there is an elegant single-span bridge.

With the arrival of railways Upton's trade rapidly declined; by the middle of the 19th century many of the warehouses were empty and there was much unemployment until the town focused on agriculture.

There are many interesting old pubs in the town. One (the White Lion) was used by Henry Fielding in his novel *Tom Jones*. It was also at this hostelry that the celebrated Mrs Siddons once acted. My favourite, however, is the Swan near the old bridge site. It is so pleasant on a sunny day to sit on the terrace and see the river craft pass by.

The Swan specialises in Banks's beer and is open all day from 11 am. There is always a full menu and the 'Specials of the Day'. The potato skins amply filled with a cheese and bacon topping are delicious and children love the Millennium Chicken Bugs with the essential chips. Telephone: 01684 592299.

- **HOW TO GET THERE:** Upton-upon-Severn is about 9 miles south of Worcester along the A38.
- **PARKING:** There is a free car park opposite the new (1878) spired church at the west end of the town.
- **LENGTH OF THE WALK:** 3 miles. Map: OS Landranger 150 Worcester and The Malverns (GR 851402).

THE WALK

1. From the car park walk to the main road, cross and turn right. Within 200 yards turn left along Minge Lane. At a crossroads turn right (Rectory Road). Within ½ mile the road twists sharp left. Turn right along Bury End which is signed as a no through road. Follow the lane to the farm at the end.

2. Keep ahead past a Dutch barn (on the right) to go through a metal

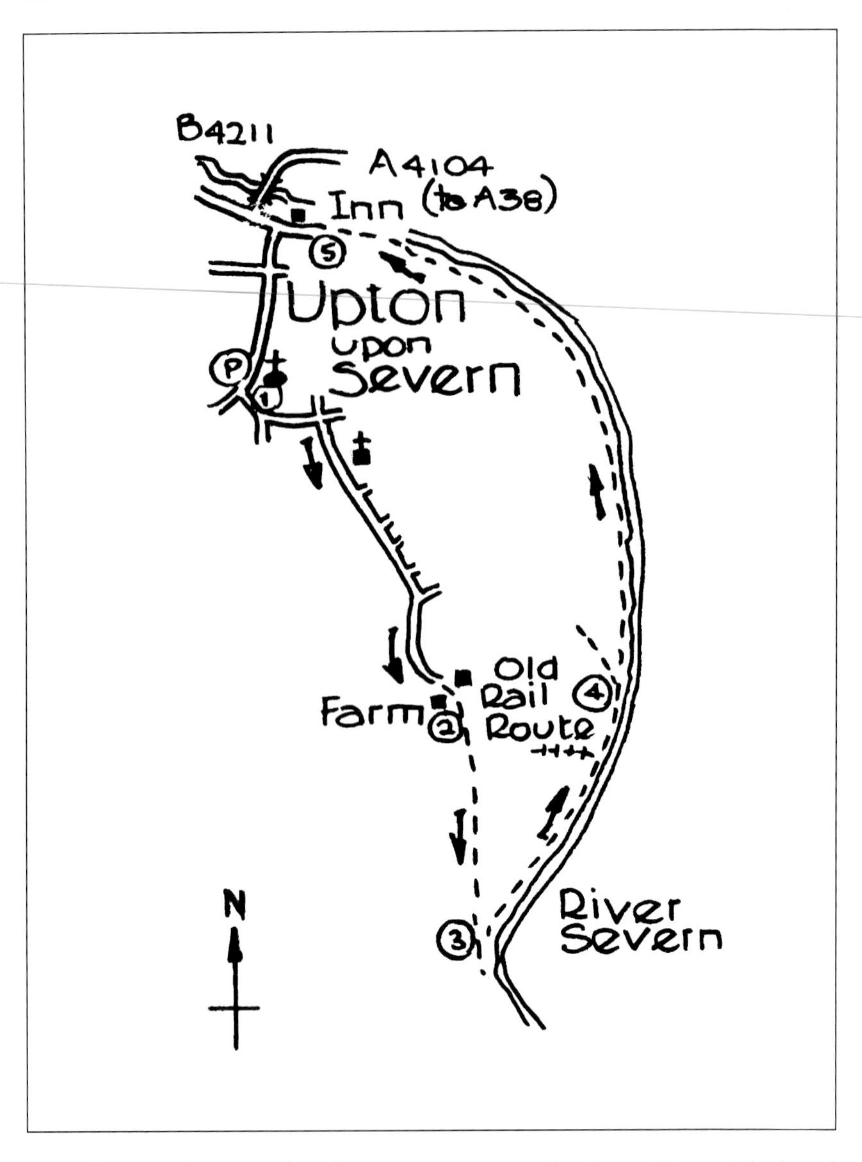

gate (waymark arrow here). In a pasture walk alongside a right-hand hedge for 200 yards. Climb a stile then regain the old heading now by a left-hand hedge.

Near a corner climb a fence stile to a large meadow. Walk by a dead oak tree and continue over an old hedge line to a step stile in a horse jump. Maintain the heading to a stile at the very far end of the field.

The 'salt-cellar' tower is all that remains of the old church in Upton-upon-Severn

3. Here we meet the river and turn left, so walking alongside the Severn. We come to a river control office on the other bank with high cables crossing the water. To the left is a long high bank – it looks like a very ancient earthwork but is in fact the line of an old railway embankment.

4. We come to a stile to climb and two paths are signed. Take the right-hand way to stay by the riverside. We are now in an SSSI – a Site of Special Scientific Interest – guarded by English Nature because of the wonderful meadow grasses and flowers. After about a mile buildings are neared and a lane is reached.

5. Keep ahead to pass the Swan. At the main street turn left to the car park.

PLACES OF INTEREST NEARBY

Tewkesbury is 6 miles to the south. The great Norman abbey church with its fine tower has overlooked the town for more than 800 years. Because the townspeople shared the place of worship with the monks it was spared the normal fate of the monasteries. There are two historical bridges in the town. One is King John's bridge and made of stone; the other is of iron and built by Thomas Telford with a span of 176 ft. *Little Malvern* is 5 miles west along the A4104 from Upton-upon-Severn. Behind the Catholic church below his beloved Malvern Hills is the grave of England's greatest composer Sir Edward Elgar.